Upgrade Your Teaching
UNDERSTANDING by DESIGN MEETS ▸ NEUROSCIENCE

Other ASCD publications by the authors:

Brain-Friendly Strategies for the Inclusion Classroom, by Judy Willis

Essential Questions: Opening Doors to Student Understanding, by Jay McTighe and Grant Wiggins

The Formative Assessment Learning Cycle (Quick Reference Guide), by Susan M. Brookhart and Jay McTighe

Learning to Love Math: Teaching Strategies That Change Student Attitudes and Get Results, by Judy Willis

Research-Based Strategies to Ignite Student Learning: Insights from a Neurologist and Classroom Teacher, by Judy Willis

Schooling by Design: Mission, Action, and Achievement, by Grant Wiggins and Jay McTighe

Solving 25 Problems in Unit Design: How do I refine my units to enhance student learning? (ASCD Arias), by Jay McTighe and Grant Wiggins

Teaching the Brain to Read: Strategies for Improving Fluency, Vocabulary, and Comprehension, by Judy Willis

Understanding by Design, expanded 2nd ed., by Grant Wiggins and Jay McTighe

The Understanding by Design Guide to Advanced Concepts in Creating and Reviewing Units, by Grant Wiggins and Jay McTighe

The Understanding by Design Guide to Creating High-Quality Units, by Grant Wiggins and Jay McTighe

Using Understanding by Design in the Culturally and Linguistically Diverse Classroom, by Amy J. Heineke and Jay McTighe

Upgrade Your Teaching

UNDERSTANDING by DESIGN MEETS NEUROSCIENCE

JAY McTIGHE

JUDY WILLIS, M.D.

ASCD

Alexandria, Virginia USA

ASCD®
1703 N. Beauregard St. • Alexandria, VA 22311-1714 USA
Phone: 800-933-2723 or 703-578-9600 • Fax: 703-575-5400
Website: www.ascd.org • E-mail: member@ascd.org
Author guidelines: www.ascd.org/write

All web links in this book are correct as of the publication date below but may have become inactive or otherwise modified since that time. If you notice a deactivated or changed link, please e-mail books@ascd.org with the words "Link Update" in the subject line. In your message, please specify the web link, the book title, and the page number on which the link appears.

PAPERBACK ISBN: 978-1-4166-2734-0 ASCD product #119008
PDF E-BOOK ISBN: 978-1-4166-2736-4; see Books in Print for other formats.
Quantity discounts: 10–49, 10%; 50+, 15%; 1,000+, special discounts (e-mail programteam@ascd.org or call 800-933-2723, ext. 5773, or 703-575-5773). For desk copies, go to www.ascd.org/deskcopy.

ASCD Member Book No. FY19-6 (Apr. 2019 PSI+). ASCD Member Books mail to Premium (P), Select (S), and Institutional Plus (I+) members on this schedule: Jan, PSI+; Feb, P; Apr, PSI+; May, P; Jul, PSI+; Aug, P; Sep, PSI+; Nov, PSI+; Dec, P. For current details on membership, see www.ascd.org/membership.

Library of Congress Cataloging-in-Publication Data
Names: McTighe, Jay, author. | Willis, Judy, author.
Title: Upgrade your teaching : understanding by design meets neuroscience / Jay McTighe, Judy Willis, M.D.
Description: Alexandria, Virginia : ASCD, [2019] | Includes bibliographical references and index.
Identifiers: LCCN 2018055822 (print) | LCCN 2019002697 (ebook) | ISBN 9781416627364 (PDF) | ISBN 9781416627340 (pbk.)
Subjects: LCSH: Learning, Psychology of. | Neurosciences.
Classification: LCC LB1060 (ebook) | LCC LB1060 .M433 2019 (print) | DDC 370.15/23—dc23
LC record available at https://lccn.loc.gov/2018055822

26 25 24 23 22 21 20 19 2 3 4 5 6 7 8 9 10 11 12

Upgrade Your Teaching

UNDERSTANDING BY DESIGN MEETS NEUROSCIENCE

We dedicate this book to the memory
of Dr. Grant Wiggins (1950–2015),
whose ideas are alive within.

We also dedicate this book to our
grandchildren—Gretel, Gus, Hendrix,
and Sage—with the hope that their school
experiences reflect the ideas we offer.

Introduction

Imagine that you are a builder who has been contracted to construct a high-rise building. You would not simply order a bunch of building materials and have the workers go at it. Instead, you would start by meeting with the clients to find out what they want and need in the building and then with the architect who will develop a detailed blueprint of the proposed structure. The blueprint provides a concrete vision of the building and guides the construction workers as they build.

As educators, we are builders of knowledge—cognitive contractors, if you will. Accordingly, we must think of our students as our clients and begin by considering what their brains need and want in order for them to effectively construct knowledge. Then we need a blueprint to guide our construction of the curriculum, the associated assessments, and the necessary learning experiences to bring the vision to life. Understanding by Design (UbD) offers such a framework. Although the UbD framework was originally conceived in the 1990s to reflect the understanding about learning emanating from cognitive psychology, it is now also supported by emerging insights from neuroscience about how the human brain best learns.

Like two streams merging into a river, this book presents the confluence of neuroscience research with the Understanding by Design framework to offer educators a unique blueprint to use in guiding students' construction of knowledge. The book begins with two introductory chapters. The first provides an overview of the neuroscience of learning, and the second provides an overview of the principles and practices of the UbD framework. Subsequent chapters describe their intersection. As you explore the UbD process for curriculum, assessment, and instructional design, you'll simultaneously be guided to construct and deepen your own understanding of the brain processes that you are facilitating at each stage of backward design—and your students will be the beneficiaries as their knowledge and understanding increase.

1

How the Brain Learns Best

The brain is always changing, as a result of environment and experience. Every lesson, assignment, and interaction shapes your students' brains. Understanding how the brain converts information into learning provides keys to the best instructional strategies and learning experiences.

As a result of breakthroughs in neuroscience research, including neuroimaging and neuroelectric monitoring of neurons (brain cells) firing, we now can observe how the brain responds during learning. These technologies provide visible representations of the brain's response to instructional practices, revealing neurological activity as information travels from the body's sensory intake systems through the attention and emotional filters, forming memory linkages and activating the highest cognitive networks of executive function. This research has illuminated our understanding of how various factors—classroom environment, activation of prior knowledge, attention-getting techniques, use of graphic organizers, mental manipulations, and others—influence the transformation of sensory information into networks of durable long-term memory and conceptual understanding.

As you build your knowledge of the strategies that promote optimal brain processing, you'll recognize that neuroscience research may well support strategies you've already found most successful in your experience as an educator. Our goal is to help you increase your understanding of why "best practice" strategies and tools work at the neurological level.

The RAS: The Brain's Attention Filter

All learning begins with sensory information. Our brains are constantly bombarded with information from the body's sensory receptors. Continuous data reports flow from specialized sensory systems (hearing, vision, taste, touch, smell) and from the sensory nerve endings in our muscles, joints, and internal organs. These receptors do not evaluate the data. They just transmit constant status reports. Of the millions of bits of sensory data available each second, only about 1 percent are admitted to the brain, whose various areas are associated with different functions, as shown in Figure 1.1. Once information enters the brain's processing systems, it is relayed by numerous "switching stations." Ultimately, conscious or higher-level processing takes place in the outer covering of the brain, called the *cortex*.

Figure 1.1 Functional Areas of the Brain

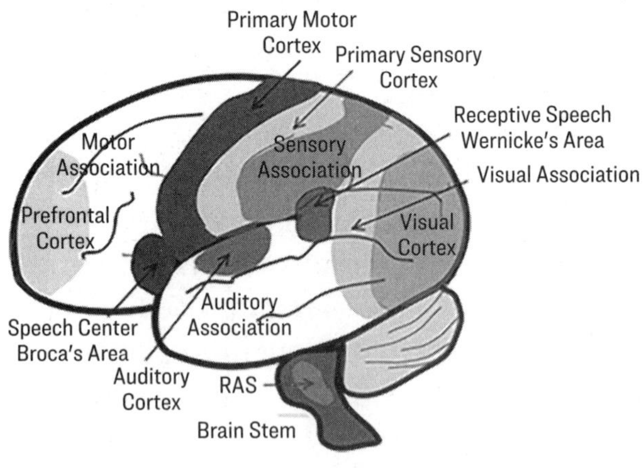

One reason for restricting the enormous amount of sensory input is that the brain is rather stingy with its mental effort because it needs to preserve its limited fuel. Unlike other organs, it has no stored nutrients or oxygen. The average brain weighs only about three pounds, but it is so dense and metabolically active that it requires over 20 percent of all the oxygen and nutrients the body consumes. From a survival standpoint, it makes good sense for the brain to be a couch potato!

Because it is impossible for the brain to consciously sort through all the sensory information that is available every second, it is programmed to prefer selected input. To deal with this selection, the brain has a sensory intake filter, called the *reticular activating system* (RAS), in the lower part of the posterior brain (see Figure 1.1). The RAS determines what the brain attends to and what information gets in. Its involuntary programming gives priority to sensory information that is most critical for mammals to survive in the unpredictable wild. Any change in the expected pattern can signal a threat of death or, alternatively, a source of nutrients that can help ensure survival. This "hard-wired" criterion of selection for entry is essentially the same for humans as for other mammals; the brain gives priority admission to sensory input about change in the expected pattern—what is new, different, changed, unexpected.

Students are often criticized for not paying attention, but we now know that failure to focus on a teacher's instruction does not mean the student's brain is inattentive. A student's RAS is always paying attention to (letting in) sensory input—but not necessarily the input being taught at that time.

The Amygdala: The Brain's Switching Station

Deep within the brain is the emotionally responsive *limbic system*, which includes two structures (one on each side of the brain) called the *amygdalae*, which direct communication between the *lower brain* and the *upper brain* (Figure 1.2). The lower brain is the more primitive control center that directs bodily functions that are largely automatic, such as breathing and digestion, as well as reactions that are largely involuntary, such as the *fight-or-flight* response. The upper brain, known as the *prefrontal cortex* (see Figure 1.1), is where memory is constructed and neural networks of executive functions guide voluntary behavior with reflective, rather than reactive, choices.

The amygdala can be thought of as the switching station for traffic flow between these upper and lower structures in the brain. After sensory information is selected to enter through the RAS, the level of activity taking place in the amygdala determines whether the information will travel down to the lower, involuntary, reactive brain or up to the reflective and memory-storing "thinking brain" (the prefrontal cortex).

Figure 1.2 The Brain's Limbic System

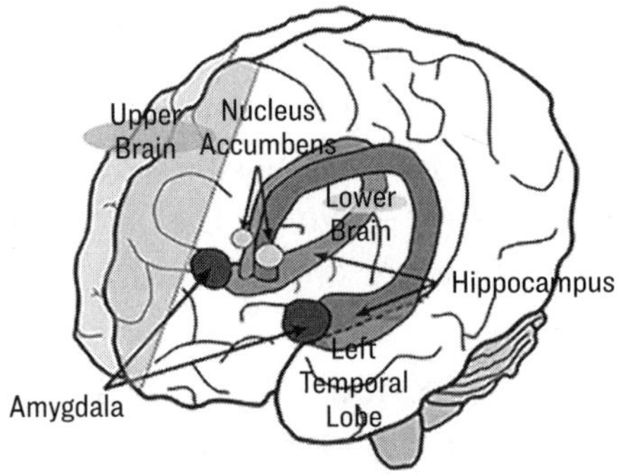

Information perceived as possibly threatening is directed through the amygdala to the reactive lower brain. Input passing through the amygdala to the prefrontal cortex finds the home of logical thought, judgment, emotional self-management, and other executive functions needed to generate more accurate predictions about new information and direct more considered responses.

When a mammal is in a state of actual or perceived stress, new information does not freely pass through the amygdala's filter to gain access to the prefrontal cortex. Instead, input is diverted to the lower, reactive brain, which has a limited set of behavioral responses that can be summarized as involuntary survival responses to a perceived threat. In fact, it is these primitive mammalian responses that we are likely to observe in students when they are highly stressed by fear, frustration (e.g., as a result of repeated failure to succeed in a task or subject), alienation, anxiety, or sustained boredom (e.g., when they are asked to do lessons or drills on topics they have already mastered or that they see as irrelevant). Here are some examples of specific school-related stressors that can trigger the amygdala to send input to the lower, reactive brain:

- Anxiety related to speaking in class, answering questions, or oral presentations
- Fear of being wrong
- Physical and language differences
- Test-taking anxiety
- Boredom as a result of prior mastery or absence of personal relevance to the material
- Frustration with material students believe exceeds their understanding
- Feeling overwhelmed by the demands of school assignments
- Inability to effectively organize time in response to the demands of academics, extracurricular activities, and out-of-school chores and jobs
- Feelings of isolation or lack of acceptance by peers or teachers

During these states of stress, students are likely to display involuntary lower-brain responses, manifested in acting-out or zoning-out behaviors.

The Brain and Mindset

Because the brain seeks to preserve its limited energy resources, it directs its behaviors based on the probability that the effort expended will result in success. Understanding this survival programming provides new perspective about students' choices and responses. It is now evident that low intelligence, lack of initiative, or laziness may not be the most likely reasons students don't always remain fully attentive, remember everything they are taught, persevere at tasks, or manage their emotions. A more fundamental explanation for nonproductive student behaviors is rooted in the brain's design, which focuses sensory intake, reacts to stress with survival responses, preserves its resources, and minimizes outputs of effort.

The brain's expenditure of voluntary effort is linked to the expectation of positive outcomes. If students fail after repeated efforts to achieve goals and academic challenges, their willingness to put forth effort will decline. These negative self-expectations can grow progressively year after year with repeated failures, further compromising the likelihood of academic success. Psychologist Carol Dweck (2007) has coined the phrase *fixed mindset* to characterize the conviction of those learners who do not believe that their effort can lead to achievement and is therefore fruitless. This contrasts with a *growth mindset,* which attributes success to effort, perseverance, and use of strategies.

In survival terms, withholding effort when past experiences predict failure is beneficial for animals in the wild. Consider a fox living in a region where prey is limited and whose den is surrounded by three hills. One of those hills is particularly steep and covered by dense underbrush where the prey hides. To repeatedly chase prey up that hill is to exert effort—in this case, energy—without the likelihood of achieving the goal of an energy-restoring meal. In the interest of survival, the fox's brain ultimately develops a mindset that deters it from chasing prey up that particular hill.

As students' efforts toward achieving a goal repeatedly fail, they might develop the fixed mindset that their intelligence and skills are predetermined, limited, and unchangeable. They become less likely to expend the effort necessary to persevere on challenging learning tasks, and they fall behind academically. Without the needed foundation of knowledge and skills to understand subsequent instruction, the gap widens further and they become even more susceptible to the stress-related blockades.

Seeking Patterns to Make Predictions

The brain's programming promotes survival of the animal and the species. This programming has guided mammalian development and adaptations for survival in the unpredictable and perilous environments in which most mammals live. The human brain continues to follow two prime survival directives: to seek *patterns* and *pleasure*. These directives drive the brain's memory, effort, and actions.

Patterning refers to the brain's meaningful categorization and organization of sensory data based on relationships or commonalities. The brain stores new information by linking it to patterns of related information already stored in neural circuits of existing memory. These clusters of related information stored together in memory are what psychologist Jean Piaget (1957) described as cognitive frameworks, or *schemas*.

It is through this pattern matching with previously constructed and related neural networks that our brains recognize and make meaning of the thousands of bits of sensory input received every second. By linking information newly stored in memory networks with relevant prior knowledge, the brain can sift through the barrage of ongoing input to make sense of the world. Storing information in memory by relationship patterning allows for easier, more efficient retrieval of information, which is essential to interpreting and predicting, and enacting the best response to something new.

All animals must make predictions to survive. For example, based on frequent links between cold temperatures and the behavior of the local rabbits in its hunting territory, a fox's brain might establish a memory pattern. The memory would result from frequent repetition of the pattern of cold temperatures linked to rabbits entering their dens earlier in the evening. Therefore, on a cold evening, the fox might predict that the time to catch its dinner is earlier than usual, perhaps just as the sun goes down.

When presented with novel sensory input, such as change, unfamiliar questions, or choices, our brains rapidly self-scan the related patterns for those that match the new information. Our brains activate these stored memories to relate to the new input and to make predictions and choose actions guided by those memory patterns.

Prediction is successful whenever the brain activates enough information from a patterned memory category to interpret the pattern of the new input. For example, if you see the number sequence 2, 4, 6, 8..., you predict the next number will be 10 because you recognize the pattern of counting by twos. Depending on the result of the prediction, the existing patterns relied upon to make the prediction are extended, fortified, or revised.

Through observations, experiences, and feedback, the brain increasingly learns about the world and can make progressively more accurate predictions about what will come next and how to respond to new information, problems, or choices. This ability for prediction, guided by pattern recognition, is a foundation for successful literacy, numeracy, test taking, appropriate social-emotional behavior, and understanding.

Successful prediction is one of the brain's best problem-solving strategies. To ensure that we will repeat the actions arising from accurate predictions, the experience of making accurate predictions stimulates a pleasure response mediated through the release of the neurochemical *dopamine*.

Dopamine: The Brain's Pleasure Drug

If you know pleasure, you know dopamine. Seeking and experiencing pleasure are innate survival features of the brain. When dopamine is released throughout the brain, it promotes feelings of pleasure, a deep satisfaction, and a drive to continue or repeat the actions that triggered the pleasurable response.

You might already be familiar with dopamine in its other function as a neurotransmitter. Neurotransmission involves *axons* and *dendrites*, two kinds of extensions of neurons that act as senders and receivers, respectively, of neural electrical signals. Dopamine carries these signals from the axons of one neuron, across a liquid-filled gap called a *synapse*, to the dendrites of another neuron.

The action of dopamine that is relevant to the pleasure or reward response derives from triggers that stimulate its release from a holding center called the *nucleus accumbens*, found near the amygdala (see Figure 1.2). This increase in circulating dopamine is seen in all mammals and activates those feelings you experience as intrinsic pleasure and satisfaction.

Making correct predictions is one of the strongest dopamine elevators. The dopamine-reward response to making accurate predictions promotes survival in mammals because the intrinsic pleasure that comes from accurate predictions drives the brain to remember and use memory circuits that have guided previously successful predictions. Experiencing accurate predictions and the resulting satisfaction of goal achievement leads the brain to remember the related choices, behaviors, actions, decisions, and responses and to seek more opportunities to repeat them. Concomitant effects include enhanced attentive focus, motivation, curiosity, memory, persistence, and perseverance.

There are intrinsic impediments to optimally processing learning through the brain. As you've read, the RAS and the amygdala are filters programmed to determine what information gets through and where it is directed.

To further optimize students' success in school, you can engage the dopamine-reward response to motivate the brain to put forth the mental effort needed for new learning. This is true even for things that are not immediately recognized as relevant or pleasurable. Academic effort can be stimulated by tapping into the brain's programming to focus attention and apply effort when pleasure is the anticipated expectation.

By showing students that they have the power to improve and by providing opportunities for them to see progress toward goals, they'll come to understand that their own effort may control the outcome. In subsequent chapters we'll suggest strategies for enhancing student engagement; reducing stress; boosting memory, motivation, and perseverance; and promoting growth (versus fixed) mindsets designed with the dopamine-reward response in mind.

The Brain's Neuroplasticity

A long-held misconception asserted that brain growth stops with birth, only to be followed by a lifetime of brain-cell death. Now we know that although most of the neurons where information is stored are present at birth, there is lifelong growth and expansion of the abundant connections through which neurons communicate. *Neuroplasticity* refers to the brain's continuous capacity to generate new neural networks in response to stimuli.

The expression "neurons that fire together, wire together" refers to the process by which the brain constructs neural networks. The increased strength of the connections between neurons that sustain memory derives from the repeated activations of those networks. Every recalled memory or memory-directed pattern activates electrical signals (firing) from neuron to neuron to stimulate a constructive process that strengthens the memory circuit. This is an aspect of neuroplasticity—the enhancement or modification of memory networks through repeated activation. (See Figure 1.3.)

The neuroplastic response includes the building of more neuronal connections as well as the thickening of the layers of insulation, called *myelin*, around existing connections. A greater number of connections among neurons in a circuit means faster and more durable communication efficiency, just as adding lanes to a highway improves traffic flow. The addition of layers of myelin around the axons increases the speed of information travel and protects the circuit from being easily eroded through disuse.

Figure 1.3 The Neuroplastic Response

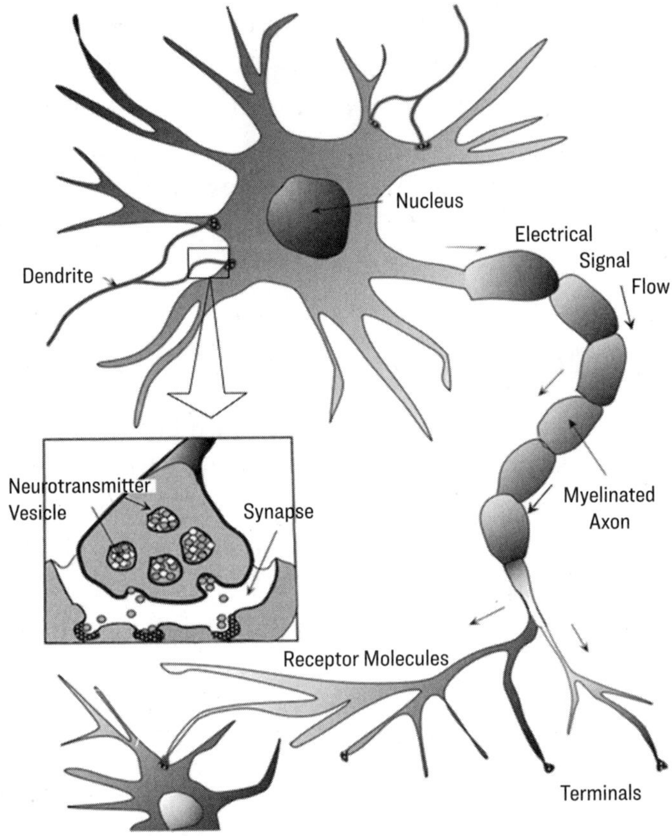

Through the neuroplastic response, the brain strengthens the circuits used most frequently, enhancing their speed. Strengthening and speeding neuron-to-neuron communication provides longer-term durability and access—that is, memories are accessed and retrieved more efficiently and they last longer. For example, when children are learning to tie their shoes, they repeatedly practice the steps. In so doing, the associated neurons repeatedly activate in sequence, strengthening the circuit of connected neurons each time. Practice results in the establishment of a "shoe-tying" network. The abundance of dendrites, enhanced by thick layers of insulating myelin around the axons, allows that behavior to become increasingly efficient and, eventually, automatic. Through neuroplasticity, the brain is molded by experience to reshape and reorganize itself so that we awake with a "new" brain each morning!

Another side of neuroplasticity, beyond building and strengthening myelinated connections, is known colloquially as the "use it or lose it" phenomenon. Without the stimulation of the electrical activity generated by use of a network, there is a gradual loss of connecting dendrites and thinning of the myelin, eventually leading to their dissolution, or pruning. Teachers are familiar with this mental pruning in a form that is often referred to as the "summer slump." Without regular use, students are likely to "forget" what had been previously taught and will require considerable review and even reteaching to reacquire their previous learning. Another example of pruning is experienced when we don't remember the foreign language we studied in high school if we don't use it regularly.

Although it may seem unproductive for the brain to prune things that have been learned, recall the brain's high metabolic demands. Without this pruning, the brain's limited resources would be spread too thin to support its efficient operation.

The major roadways of neuron-to-neuron connections are in the cerebral cortex, and there are not many branching connections between them. The pattern is comparable to a view of the major cross-country highways from five miles above Earth, without the side streets. The filling in of the brain's cognitive map takes place over time as students actively engage in mental manipulations of information. Key learning activities planned through the curriculum planning framework Understanding by Design (described in the next chapter), such as exploring essential questions and engaging in authentic tasks, build and expand the cognitive networks needed for conceptual understanding and transfer.

How the Brain Remembers

New memory construction takes place after new sensory information leaves the amygdala and enters a brain structure called the *hippocampus* (see Figure 1.2), whose name derives from the Greek word for *seahorse*, because of its resemblance to that creature. This structure is where new sensory intake connects to a bit of pre-existing memory and consolidates from immediate into short-term memory.

None of our memories are held in single neurons. It has been a momentous evolutionary extension that has enabled communication among hundreds and thousands of neurons, each holding tiny memory pieces, to recall even the simplest concept or perform the most basic tasks, such as clapping one's hands.

Memory is stored in separate hemispheres of the brain, based on the sensory modality (e.g., vision or hearing) in which it is experienced. These multiple storage areas are linked by dendrites and axons (see Figure 1.3). The brain develops stronger and extended memory circuits when new learning is connected to multiple circuits by recognizing the common threads among existing circuits or experiencing the learning through multiple sensory modalities, such as vision, hearing, and movement.

Here's an example: If students learn about the positive and negative charges of magnets and relate the information to other memory circuits that include the concepts of positive and negative (evident in things such as emotions, electricity, numbers, or economic influences), they will store and can retrieve what they learned about magnets through multiple pathways. If positive and negative magnetic forces are further related to a story in which opposites attract, thinking about that story can retrieve an even more detailed memory of facts related to magnets.

Storage of memory in neural networks based on patterns (relationships) has evolved into a very effective system in which the brain accesses prior knowledge to enable it to make connections to new information and situations. For example, memory based on patterns and relationships guides children to avoid objects designated as hot. It takes only one or two negative experiences of feeling the discomfort of touching a hot stove or campfire, along with hearing the word *hot* or seeing flames, for their brains to construct the relational memory cementing the notion that the word *hot* stands for things that should not be touched. In short, they learn.

Have you ever read aloud a familiar story or poem and left out a word or phrase that is often repeated or rhymed? If so, it is likely that children have jumped in to complete that sentence. Their action reflects the brain's use of patterning. In mathematics, pattern recognition is what allows students to predict the next number in a sequence or to recognize which procedure to apply when word problems use phrases such as *all together, remaining,* or *left over*.

Activating students' existing relevant prior knowledge takes place when they understand a framework into which the new learning belongs. This awareness guides the brain to recognize connections with existing memory networks in the hippocampus. Knowing how the brain makes connections can help teachers maximize learning in their classrooms, especially because students themselves do not always make connections between what they already know and new information being taught.

To ensure that there is related existing memory in the hippocampus to link with the new input, it is essential to help students become aware of their prior knowledge. When new information is presented with some foundational pattern recognized by the brain, memory networks incorporate it more efficiently. For example, when students are learning about triangles, you can start by reminding them about other shapes with which they are already familiar, such as squares and circles. Illustrating how a square can be cut or folded to create a triangle and how two equal triangles can be put together to create a square will promote the linking of the new (triangle) to the known (square). With a successful pattern match, the new information encodes into a short-term memory circuit. Strategies to ensure activation of prior knowledge include the use of pre-assessments, advance organizers, essential questions, concept maps, graphic organizers, and "hook" activities. (These and related strategies will be described in greater detail in later chapters.) Such strategies make it more likely that students will link the new information to their prior knowledge to both consolidate and expand memory circuits.

Long-Term and Concept Memory Construction

Not all activations of memory circuits stimulate the neuroplastic response equally. Less neuroplastic growth occurs if circuits are activated only by multiple repetitions of the same information in the same format—for example, writing a word 10 times or solving 30 equations using the same formula. Rote memorization produces isolated and somewhat feeble circuits unlinked to other networks. Such shallow memories only allow learners to "give back" what was taught, mirroring the way it was taught. This limits their ability to transfer—that is, to apply their learning to new situations beyond the original context in which it was learned.

Once encoded, short-term memory requires mental manipulation of the new information—it must be thought about or applied—to form richer and deeper connections and ensure its place in long-term memory storage. Without this mental manipulation, the short-term memory fades in less than a minute. Indeed, practice really does make permanent, as long as the practice involves active mental manipulation, construction of new ideas, and opportunities to apply the newly acquired knowledge and skills in different ways than they were originally learned—all tenets of the UbD framework.

The Video Game Model

What can we do to motivate sustained effort from a stingy brain and improve the mindset of students, especially those who have experienced failure and the erosion of their confidence in school? To answer this question, consider an activity that is popular among many young people and that leads them, despite repeated failures, to persevere—video games!

The video game experience models effective learning by the brain and thus offers a guide for effective teaching strategies. We have identified four elements of this model that educators can replicate to enhance the learning of their students: (1) establishing a desirable goal, (2) offering an achievable challenge, (3) providing constant assessment with specific feedback, and (4) acknowledging progress and achievement en route to a final goal.

Desirable Goals

Whether it is saving Earth from a devastating asteroid collision, slaying a dragon, or finding a lost treasure, a video game player knows the ultimate goal of the game. Players participate in the game because they enjoy the challenge or because friends or other people who are playing think it's cool. They buy into the goal of the game, even though it is merely fantasy.

Similarly, in the classroom, we need to make clear at the beginning of a new unit what the goals are and what it will take to achieve them. The brain's self-preservation programming means that it is most likely to apply its resources when it recognizes that effort will help to attain a desired goal. Accordingly, students will be more likely to engage and make an effort when they have clarity about the learning goal, evidence of its achievement, and an understanding of how a particular goal relates to them. In other words, goal buy-in is a critical component for all learning in order to motivate the brain to focus its attention, apply its energy resources, and persist when challenges arise. Like those that motivate avid video game players, goals need to be clear and relevant for students to have goal buy-in.

Achievable Challenges

Imagine the following scenarios:

- You are dropped off at the top of a ski resort's steepest run when you are only a beginner.
- You must spend your day on the bunny hill when you are an expert skier.
- You play a game of darts with the target 2 feet away.
- You play a game of darts with the target 20 feet away.
- You are a 3rd grade student trying to complete a crossword puzzle designed for adults.
- You are an adult trying to do a crossword puzzle designed for young children.

In each of these extremes, you would likely feel either frustrated or bored, depending on your level of mastery in relation to the challenge. Reflecting on those feelings helps us understand the stress students feel if they do not have the foundational knowledge to understand new topics or the skills required by a challenging task. Alternatively, consider how bored you feel when you are asked to spend time on a topic or skill that you have already mastered.

Engaging video games are designed around levels of difficulty (such as 1 to 10) and require progression through appropriate levels of challenge based on player mastery. When playing a game, players are usually working on a task at their appropriate challenge level and can progress only after achieving it. This same model of allowing game players to progress according to their individualized levels of achievable challenge is a key to reducing stress and sustaining motivated effort in the classroom.

Achievable challenge means that learning goals are clear and the learner embraces the expectation that success or mastery is within reach. Applying the video game model to classroom learning means planning goals that students accept as being within their range of potential. The famed Russian cognitive psychologist Lev Vygotsky (1978) coined the phrase *zone of proximal development* to characterize the importance of finding the balance point between learning tasks that are not at all challenging and those that are out of reach. When learners have opportunities to work toward desirable goals at their individualized levels of achievable challenge, their brains invest more effort in the task, remain more responsive to corrective feedback, and engage with the focus and perseverance akin to that of video gamers. As Goldilocks would say, the challenge needs to be "not too hard, not too easy, but just right!"

Constant Assessment with Specific Feedback

A central feature of video games is their feedback system. Players receive constant feedback as they play; they can then use that feedback to immediately make adjustments, alter their actions, and find out if these are successful. Gamers certainly make errors (incorrect predictions) on the way to mastery, but the most compelling games give feedback and unlimited chances to try again without pressure or the stress of boredom or hopeless frustration. When their choice or prediction is wrong, they know they will always have another chance. Solo players aren't receiving the negative message that they are alone in their confusion or experiencing the boredom of waiting for a class full of others playing the same game to catch up to their level before proceeding. Without those stressors, they remain comfortable trying other strategies or building skills needed for the designated task. Through experience, they find that despite frequent errors, if they act on feedback and persist, they will eventually improve and make incremental progress toward their goals. This cycle reinforces a growth mindset.

When the brain receives the feedback on progress that has been made, the associated memory, skill, or concept networks are reinforced. You can emulate the video game model in the classroom by providing your students with regular and timely feedback from formative assessments. The benefits of this practice have been conclusively documented (Black & Wiliam, 1998).

Acknowledgment of Progress and Achievement

It is interesting to note that video game players fail to achieve their goal as much as 80 percent of the time while playing. Why, then, do they persevere? Note that video games do not require mastery of all tasks at all levels; instead they highlight incremental progress. A player's advancement is noted via points, tokens, or graphics. Neurologically, each time a player's progress is acknowledged in the game, a small dopamine release occurs in the player's brain.

The motivation to persevere and pursue greater challenge at the next level stems from the brain seeking another surge of dopamine, which is the fuel of intrinsic reinforcement. This explains why players seek greater challenge at the next level. To keep the pleasure of intrinsic reinforcement going, the brain needs a higher level of challenge, because remaining at a level already mastered does not activate the necessary expectation of dopamine and its pleasure.

Much of what makes video games so compelling is the way they continuously give players evidence of the efficacy of their practice and continued efforts—essential ingredients for development of a growth mindset. The academic learning model can follow suit. When learners have opportunities to engage in learning tasks at their individualized, achievable levels of challenge and believe that their effort can achieve the goal, they are more likely to persist. When incremental progress is valued, they are more likely to recognize that specific feedback will help them improve toward goal achievement, rather than seeing the feedback as criticism or evidence of failure.

The video game model gets at the essence of building growth mindsets fueled by the belief that performance and achievement can improve by using feedback and exerting effort. Students build the self-confidence and experience the intrinsic satisfaction needed to persevere and confront successive challenges.

In subsequent chapters, we will explore the use of the UbD framework for planning curriculum, assessment, and instruction that support how the brain learns best.

Chapter Understandings

- The past two decades of brain research have provided insights that have profoundly extended our understanding of how to maximize

the brain's development of the neural networks known as executive functions, the foundation for building skills. This research can be applied to optimize learning success.
- Because it is impossible for the brain to consciously sort through all the sensory information available every second, the brain has an attention filter that prioritizes what information gets in.
- The amygdalae are switching stations that direct communication between the lower brain and the upper brain.
- The brain seeks patterns. Pattern recognition enables predictions. Pattern linking builds short-term memory, and activation of prior knowledge promotes this memory linkage.
- Durable long-term memory and enduring understanding are promoted by active mental manipulations, construction of new ideas, and opportunities to apply newly acquired knowledge and skills in different ways than they were originally learned.
- Dopamine is a neurotransmitter that is released when a learner makes a successful prediction, reaches a goal, or makes progress toward a goal. When dopamine is released in the brain, it promotes feelings of pleasure, a deep satisfaction, and a drive to continue or repeat the actions that triggered the pleasurable response.
- Learners with a fixed mindset do not believe that their effort can lead to achievement and are unlikely to put forth effort when challenged to learn something new. Learners with a growth mindset attribute success to effort, perseverance, and strategy use.
- The video game model contains replicable elements—goal buy-in, achievable challenge, frequent assessment with specific feedback, and acknowledgment of progress—that can be applied in the classroom to promote engaged attention, sustained effort, and perseverance.
- Every class, assignment, and experience reshapes each student's brain through neuroplasticity. Understanding how the brain processes information and changes in response to experiences provides keys to best strategies and interventions for guiding learners to sound understanding and durable, transferrable, long-term memory.

Questions and Answers

Does using the video game model in the classroom mean that students should be playing video games to learn content?

Although there may be some value in having learning games matched to students' skill levels (e.g., for developing basic math skills or learning vocabulary in a new language), that is not our point. Instead, we propose that particular components of video game design can be emulated in the classroom (without actual video games). When these components are incorporated into an instruction and assessment system, they compel students to learn and sustain effort through challenge and setbacks, and they promote motivated effort and learning.

Is dopamine always a good thing? Can students get too much dopamine from learning experiences designed to promote the dopamine-reward response?

In some addictions and types of mental illness such as schizophrenia, an excess release of dopamine has a negative impact. However, in the amounts released by the dopamine boosters we suggest to promote learning and sustain effort, dopamine will not be elevated to the levels where the effects are negative.

2

An Overview of Understanding by Design

Understanding by Design (UbD) is a curriculum planning framework that is well aligned to the ideas of brain-based education. As its title suggests, UbD reflects the convergence of two independent ideas: (1) research on learning and cognition that highlights the centrality of teaching and assessing for understanding and transfer, and (2) a time-honored process for designing curriculum.

The UbD framework is based on seven key tenets:

1. Learning is enhanced when teachers think purposefully about curriculum planning. The framework supports thoughtful curriculum design without offering a rigid process or prescriptive program.
2. The framework helps focus curriculum and teaching on the development and deepening of student understanding and transfer of learning—that is, the ability to effectively use content knowledge and skill.
3. Understanding is revealed when students can make sense of, and transfer, their learning through authentic performance. Six facets of understanding—the capacity to *explain, interpret, apply, shift perspective, empathize,* and *self-assess*—can serve as indicators of understanding.
4. Effective curriculum is planned *backward* from long-term outcomes through a three-stage design process. This process helps avoid three common educational problems: (a) treating the textbook as the curriculum rather than as a resource; (b) activity-oriented teaching in which no clear priorities and purposes are apparent; and (c) test prep, in which students practice the format

of standardized tests (usually selected-response items) while concentrating only on tested content.

5. Teachers are coaches of understanding, not mere purveyors of content knowledge, skill, or activity. They focus on ensuring that transfer of learning happens, rather than just assuming that students learned what was taught.
6. Regular reviews of curriculum against design standards enhance curricular quality, leading to deeper learning; at the same time, concomitant reviews of student work in professional learning communities (PLCs) inform needed adjustments in curriculum and instruction so that student learning is maximized.
7. Teachers, schools, and districts can "work smarter" and more effectively by sharing their curriculum and assessment designs with others—for example, through the Eduplanet21 Unit Planner (www.eduplanet21.com).

Understanding as an Educational Aim

The heading for this section may strike some people as unnecessary. Don't all teachers want their students to understand what they teach? Perhaps. But an examination of numerous classrooms reveals that instruction is often focused on superficial coverage of lots of content specified by national, state, or provincial standards, or contained in textbooks. Moreover, teaching for understanding may be undercut by the pressures associated with standardized accountability tests. Too often, teachers are expected to engage in test prep as a means of raising achievement scores. At its worst, this practice encourages multiple-choice teaching that results in superficial learning at the expense of exploring ideas in greater depth and allowing authentic applications.

Understanding by Design proposes a sound alternative to these prevailing methods. UbD is predicated on the idea that long-term achievement gains are more likely when teachers teach for understanding of transferable concepts and processes while giving learners multiple opportunities to apply their learning in meaningful and authentic contexts. The requisite knowledge and skills are learned through the process of actively constructing meaning—that is, coming to an understanding—and in transferring learning to new situations.

Support for an understanding-based approach to instruction and classroom assessment comes from research in cognitive psychology. Here are brief summaries of several findings (Bransford, Brown, & Cocking, 2000) that provide a theoretical base for the instructional and assessment practices of UbD:

- To be widely applicable, learning must be guided by generalized principles. Knowledge learned at the level of rote memory rarely transfers; transfer most likely occurs when the learner knows and understands underlying concepts and principles that can be applied to problems in new contexts. Learning with understanding is more likely to promote transfer than simply memorizing information from a text or a lecture.
- Experts first seek to develop an understanding of a problem, which often involves thinking in terms of core concepts or big ideas. Novices' knowledge is much less likely to be organized around big ideas; novices are more likely to approach a problem by searching for correct formulas and pat answers that fit their already-held conceptions.
- Research on expertise suggests that superficial coverage of many topics in the domain is a poor way to help students develop the competencies that will prepare them for future learning and work. Curricula that emphasize breadth of knowledge may prevent effective organization of knowledge because they do not allow enough time to learn anything in depth. Curricula that are "a mile wide and an inch deep" risk developing disconnected rather than connected knowledge.
- Many assessments measure only propositional (factual) knowledge and never ask for conditional knowledge—whether students know *when, where,* and *why* to use what they have learned. Given this real-world goal, assessments and feedback must focus on understanding, and not simply on memory for procedures or facts.

Additional validation of the principles and practices of UbD comes from the emerging research on the neuroscience of learning (Willis, 2006). Research results provide a conceptual underpinning for UbD and guide curriculum and assessment design, as well as instructional practice.

In Chapter 1 we explored the physiology of the brain as it relates to learning. The following are among the most salient points on how the brain learns:

- *Patterning* is the process whereby the brain perceives and generates patterns by relating new with previously learned material or chunking material into patterns it has not used before. Whenever new material is presented in such a way that students see relationships, greater brain cell activity is generated (forming new neural connections), and students can more successfully store their learning in long-term memory and retrieve it.
- Experiential learning that stimulates multiple senses in students, such as hands-on science, is not only the most engaging form of learning but also the most likely to be stored as long-term memories.
- The best-remembered information is learned through multiple and varied exposures followed by authentic uses of the knowledge.
- The neural networks that control the brain's *executive functions* are most responsive, developing and maturing at an extremely fast rate, during the school years through the mid-20s. These networks control the abilities of highest cognition, including focusing attention, critical analysis, reasoning, judgment, risk assessment, flexible and innovative thinking, emotional self-regulation, efficiency of memory, creative problem solving, and metacognitive self-management. Instruction that engages the use of these functions strengthens them.

The past two decades of brain research have provided insights that have profoundly extended our understanding of how to maximize the brain's development of the neural networks related to executive functions. These functions are exactly what students need for success in this era of surging amounts of information and rapidly transitioning technology. The school years are critical times in children's development of their sense of themselves and their relationships to the world.

The executive-function command system evolving in the prefrontal cortexes of students' brains needs experience and guidance to build the skill sets required for setting and achieving long-term goals. Teachers have the opportunity and important responsibility to guide their students' construction of the skills needed to successfully, and ultimately independently, identify goals, evaluate appropriate actions, plan goal achievement, delay immediate gratification, and use and revise strategies to realize their goals and aspirations.

What *Is* Understanding?

The term *understanding* can be tricky. Its ambiguity reflects the fact that it can be used with different connotations and intentions. In fact, you may be aware that educational psychologist Benjamin Bloom and his colleagues avoided using the term in their taxonomy of the cognitive domain because they found it imprecise (Bloom, 1956).

One way to explore the term's meaning is to consider how understanding is shown. Try the following mental exercise: Think about something you *understand* deeply, such as a subject you teach or ideas related to a hobby. Now, think about the ways in which your understanding is shown. How would others know you have that understanding? Given your understanding, what can you do that a person without that understanding cannot? When we use this exercise in workshops, participants offer predictable responses.

Indicators of Deep Understanding *You can...*	**Indicators of a Little Knowledge but Not Deep Understanding** *You can...*
• Explain things clearly and completely. • Teach others effectively. • Apply your understanding flexibly in new situations (transfer). • Analyze and evaluate information and sources. • Justify and support your ideas/positions. • Interpret meaning of things such as text, data, and experiences. • Generate new questions.	• Give back what you were told. • Plug in. • Remember. • Select the "correct" answer from given alternatives.

• Recognize different points of view on an issue. • Empathize with others. • Diagnose errors and correct them. • Self-assess and monitor your progress. • Adjust midcourse. • Reflect on your own learning.	• Apply a skill only in the way it was learned; you cannot transfer your learning to a new situation. . . . and you are less able to do the things listed under Indicators of Deep Understanding.

The indicators of deep understanding help us to "understand understanding." They not only highlight the various ways the term is used but also offer specific ideas for assessment. In other words, when we want to see if students understand a concept or process, we can ask them to do one or more of the things listed. Their response will show the extent to which they understand. Notice that the abilities related to deep understanding are associated with the brain's executive functions. Indeed, this recognition—that teaching and assessing for deep understanding builds the neural networks in the prefrontal cortex of the brain—lies at the heart of this book. At the same time, as these networks mature and expand, students' capacity to understand and transfer their learning is enriched.

In its essence, the UbD framework is intended to help educators identify the big ideas that we want students to come to understand at a deep level so that they can transfer their learning to new situations. Such ideas are inherently abstract. They take the form of concepts (e.g., *adaptation*), principles (e.g., *F=MA*), and processes (e.g., *Writers draft and revise their writing to achieve clarity of expression*).

The ability to effectively transfer knowledge and skill involves the capacity to take what we know and use it creatively, flexibly, and fluently, in different settings or with different problems. Rote learning will not equip a student for transfer. Transfer requires understanding.

A focus on student understanding and transfer does not mean that educators should ignore basic skills or refrain from teaching facts. Basic knowledge and skills are foundational. Indeed, thinking requires a knowledge base, and students cannot apply learning effectively if they lack basic skills. However, we contend that the basics should be considered the floor, not the ceiling. In an era when students can tap into much of the world's knowledge using a smartphone, it makes sense to put a greater premium on preparing them to be able to transfer their learning to new, even unpredictable, situations. In other words, schools should develop *know-how* as well as *knowing*.

The Three Stages of Backward Design

Teaching is a means to an end, and curriculum planning precedes instruction. The most successful teaching begins with clarity about desired learning outcomes *and* about the evidence that will show learning has occurred. Understanding by Design supports this view through a *backward design* process for planning curriculum units that include desired understandings and performance tasks that require transfer. Daily lessons are then developed in the context of a more comprehensive unit design. More specifically, the UbD framework offers a three-stage curriculum design process that includes a unit template, design tools that support the process, and a set of design standards for quality control. A key component of a curriculum based on the UbD framework is alignment, with all three stages clearly aligned not only to standards but also to one another.

The concept of planning curriculum *backward* from desired results is not new. In 1948, Ralph Tyler advocated this approach as an effective process for focusing instruction. William Spady (1994) popularized the idea of "designing down" from exit outcomes, and in his best-selling book *The 7 Habits of Highly Effective People*, Stephen Covey noted that effective people always plan "with the end in mind" (Covey, 1998). Although the idea is not novel, we have found that the intentional use of backward design results in more clearly defined goals, more appropriate assessments, and more purposeful teaching. The following sections provide a brief summary of the three stages of backward design used in UbD curriculum planning.

Stage 1: Identify Desired Results

In the first stage, curricular planners grapple with what they want learners to understand, know, and do at the end of the instructional unit. They consider the following questions: *What do we want students to be able to do with their learning in the long run? What should students come to understand in order for them to transfer their learning? What essential questions will students explore? What knowledge and skills will students need to acquire?*

This first stage in the design process calls for clarity about instructional priorities and long-term versus short-term goals. In Stage 1, we consider the *big ideas* we want students to come to understand and the long-term transfer goals that those ideas enable. We examine established content standards and related curriculum outcomes, such as 21st century skills, to identify the big ideas to be understood and the related transfer performances. We frame companion *essential questions* around these targeted *understandings* and *transfer goals*. Finally, we identify more specific knowledge and skill objectives.

Stage 2: Determine Acceptable Evidence

In the second stage, curriculum planners determine the evidence needed for learners to demonstrate transfer and understanding as related to the unit goals. They consider these questions: *What performances and products will reveal evidence of student understanding and ability to transfer? What additional assessment evidence will be used to assess other learning outcomes?*

Backward design encourages us to think like assessors *before* planning lesson activities in Stage 3. In other words, we think about the assessment that will show the extent to which our students have attained the learning outcomes set forth in Stage 1. It is one thing to say that students should understand X and be able to do Y; it is another to ask: What *evidence will show* that they understand X and can effectively apply Y? We have found that considering the needed assessment evidence helps focus and sharpen the learning plan in Stage 3.

Evidence of understanding is obtained through performance tasks that ask students to explain the meaning(s) they have made and to apply—to transfer—their learning to new situations. We recommend that the performance assessments be set in a meaningful and authentic context whenever possible. Supplementary assessments, such as a quiz on facts or a skills check, provide additional evidence of students' knowledge acquisition and skill proficiency.

Stage 2 of UbD embodies a fundamental *if-then* proposition: *If* you acknowledge that a primary goal of a modern education is to equip students to be able to transfer their learning to new situations, *then* you should design curriculum backward from authentic performances of transfer, not from long lists of discrete topics or skills.

Stage 3: Plan Learning Experiences and Instruction

In the third stage, curricular planners design experiences for learners to reach and demonstrate attainment of goals. They consider the following questions: *What activities, experiences, and lessons will lead to achievement of the desired results and success at the assessments? How will the learning plan help students acquire, make meaning, and transfer? How will the unit be sequenced and differentiated to optimize achievement for all learners?*

With clearly identified learning results and appropriate assessment evidence in mind, we now plan the most appropriate instructional activities for helping learners acquire targeted knowledge and skills, come to understand important ideas, and apply their learning in meaningful ways. The various types of learning goals identified in Stage 1—acquisition of knowledge and skills, understanding of big ideas, and transfer—inform the selection of instructional strategies and pedagogical roles, such as direct instructor, facilitator, and coach. In other words, instructional practices need to be aligned to the desired results (Stage 1) and their assessments (Stage 2).

We have found that when teachers follow this three-stage planning process, they are more likely to avoid the familiar "twin sins" of planning and teaching. The first sin, which occurs more widely at the elementary and middle school levels, may be labeled *activity-oriented teaching*. Teachers plan and conduct various activities that may be engaging, hands-on, and kid-friendly. These are fine qualities as long as the activities are purposefully focused on clear and important goals *and* they yield appropriate evidence of learning. However, too often the collection of activities—even engaging ones—does not add up to coherent and focused learning. Constructing a baking soda volcano in science, building an igloo out of sugar cubes in social studies, or baking a sheet cake shaped like the state of Colorado in geography are examples of well-intentioned classroom activities that are unlikely to yield deep and enduring understandings about big ideas. Such activities are like cotton candy—pleasant enough in the moment, but lacking long-term substance.

The second sin, more prevalent at the secondary and collegiate levels, goes by the name of *coverage*. In this case, teaching consists of marching chronologically through the content, often in the form of long lists of grade-level standards or material in textbooks. With all due respect to the content-related challenges of secondary teaching, a teacher's job is not to simply cover what is in a book; a teacher's job is to *uncover* the content in ways that develop and deepen students' understanding of important ideas and equip them to transfer their learning in meaningful ways. The textbook should serve as a resource, *not* as the syllabus. We have found that backward design is key to helping teachers better understand their priorities and the role of the textbook and other resources.

The Understanding by Design Unit Template

The UbD unit-planning template provides a graphic organizer that embodies the various elements of Understanding by Design and reflects the logic of backward design. Figure 2.1 presents the template with questions that teachers consider when planning a UbD unit.

When teachers first encounter UbD, especially without a thorough introduction, they may think that this approach to curriculum planning is simply a matter of filling in boxes on a template. This view confuses a tool (the unit template) with the *process* of backward design. We contend that backward design has an important logic; it reflects a way of thinking and planning to ensure clarity of outcomes, appropriate assessments, and focused teaching by always keeping the *ends* of understanding and transfer in mind.

Although completing the unit template is not the goal of UbD, the template has proven to be a valuable tool for curriculum planning. Like any effective graphic organizer, the UbD template serves as a guide to users, resulting in a "mental template" that helps teachers internalize a robust curriculum planning process. The UbD template has another virtue: its common layout enables teachers to share units in a recognizable format with other teachers throughout a school, across a district or state, and anywhere in the world!

Figure 2.1 The UbD Template with Planning Questions

<table>
<tr><td colspan="3">Stage 1—Desired Results</td></tr>
<tr><td rowspan="6">Established Goals
What content standards and program- or mission-related goal(s) will this unit address?</td><td colspan="2">Transfer</td></tr>
<tr><td colspan="2">Students will be able to independently use their learning to . . .
What kinds of long-term, independent accomplishments are desired?</td></tr>
<tr><td colspan="2">Meaning</td></tr>
<tr><td>Understandings
Students will understand that . . .
What specifically do you want students to understand?</td><td>Essential Questions
Students will keep considering . . .
What thought-provoking questions will foster inquiry, meaning making, and transfer?</td></tr>
<tr><td colspan="2">Acquisition</td></tr>
<tr><td>Students will know . . .
What facts and basic concepts should students know and be able to remember?</td><td>Students will be skilled at . . .
What discrete skills and processes should students be able to use?</td></tr>
</table>

<table>
<tr><th colspan="2">Stage 2—Evidence</th></tr>
<tr><td>Evaluative Criteria</td><td>Assessment Evidence</td></tr>
<tr><td rowspan="2">• What criteria will be used in each assessment to evaluate attainment of the desired results?
• What are the most important qualities for student performance?</td><td>Performance Task(s)
How will students demonstrate their understanding (meaning making and transfer) through transfer performance(s)?
Consider the six facets when developing assessments of understanding. Optional: Use the GRASPS* elements to frame an authentic context for the task(s).</td></tr>
<tr><td>Supplementary Evidence
What other evidence will you collect to determine whether Stage 1 goals were achieved?</td></tr>
</table>

<table>
<tr><th colspan="2">Stage 3—Learning Plan</th></tr>
<tr><td colspan="2">What pre-assessments will be used to check students' prior knowledge, skill levels, and potential misconceptions? Pre-assessment</td></tr>
<tr><td>Learning Events
• What teaching and learning experiences will be used to help students . . .
– Acquire targeted knowledge and skills?
– Make meaning of big ideas?
– Be able to transfer their learning?
• How will you help learners know the learning goals, recognize the value of this learning, and understand how their learning will be assessed?
• How will you hook and engage learners' interest?
• How will you tailor (i.e., differentiate) the learning plan to address the varied interests and achievement levels of all students?
• How will you help learners self-assess their performance, reflect on their learning, and set future goals?</td><td>Formative Assessments
• What ongoing assessments will be used to monitor students' progress toward acquisition, meaning making, and transfer throughout the unit?
• How and when will students get the feedback they need and have opportunities to make use of it?</td></tr>
</table>

Source: From *The Understanding by Design Guide to Creating High-Quality Units* (pp. 16–17), by G. Wiggins and J. McTighe, 2011, Alexandria, VA: ASCD. Copyright 2011 by Grant Wiggins and Jay McTighe. Adapted with permission.

*See p. 81 for information on GRASPS.

A Driving Example

To illustrate the backward design process in action, let's consider how UbD could be used in driver training. In Stage 1, we reference the following American Driver and Traffic Safety Education Association's national standards for driver education:

- Demonstrate a working knowledge of rules, regulations, and procedures of operating an automobile.
- Use visual search skills to obtain correct information and make reduced-risk decisions for effective speed and position adjustments.
- Interact with other users within the Highway Transportation System by adjusting speed, space, and communications to avoid conflicts and reduce risk.
- Demonstrate balanced vehicle movement through steering, braking, and accelerating in a precise and timely manner throughout a variety of adverse conditions.

We then specify the information a beginning driver will need to know, such as basic car parts and their functions, the driving rules and regulations for their jurisdiction, the meaning of traffic signs and signals, and procedures to follow in case of an accident. We would also identify the various skills a beginning driver will need to practice, including adjusting the driver's seat and car mirrors, coordinating the gas and brake pedals, signaling intentions to other drivers, merging into traffic on a highway, and parallel parking.

In addition to targeting knowledge and skills, planning with UbD also requires identifying the *big ideas* we want students to understand. Here are several understandings for driving:

- A motor vehicle can become a lethal weapon, and driving one demands constant attention to avoid damage, injuries, or death.
- Defensive driving assumes that other drivers are inattentive and might make unexpected or dangerous moves.
- Effective drivers constantly adapt their driving to various traffic, road, and weather conditions.

Notice that these are not facts, but rather conceptual understandings that guide experienced drivers in safely operating a motor vehicle.

Finally, we ask ourselves: What are the ultimate goals of a driver training program? Certainly, effective driving demands more than simply having novice drivers memorize the rules of the road and master discrete driving skills. Long-term transfer goals for driving look like these:

- Effective drivers drive courteously and defensively without accidents or needless risk.
- Effective drivers adapt their knowledge of safe driving to various traffic, road, and weather conditions.

Keeping these long-term *ends* in mind focuses teaching and learning. Indeed, a successful driver training program should be designed backward from such goals.

You may have noticed that there is one category of the Stage 1 template that we have not yet referenced in this example—*Essential Questions*. Such questions are open-ended; they do not seek a single "correct" answer. Rather, they are meant to be considered over time as a means of helping students construct meaning and deepen their understanding. Given the targeted understandings and transfer goals for driver education, here are two essential questions that could be used to frame the entire course:

- *What must I anticipate and do to minimize risk and accidents when I drive?*
- *What makes a courteous and defensive driver?*

Essential questions like these provide a conceptual umbrella for a unit or a course. They remind both teachers and students that simply acquiring information or basic skills is insufficient; the ultimate goal is transfer, and transfer requires understanding. Figure 2.2 presents this example within Stage 1 of the UbD unit template.

Let's continue examining the backward design process by moving into Stage 2 for the driver education example. In Stage 2, we ask teachers to think like an assessor, to consider the evidence needed to determine the extent to which students have achieved the identified knowledge, skills, understandings, and transfer goals specified in Stage 1. The logic of backward design asks teachers to carefully consider what these different goals imply for the assessments (in Stage 2) and then for instruction (in Stage 3).

Figure 2.2 Stage 1 of the UbD Unit Template with Driver Education Example

<table>
<tr><th colspan="3">Stage 1—Desired Results</th></tr>
<tr><th>Established Goals</th><th colspan="2">Transfer</th></tr>
<tr><td rowspan="5">National Driver Development Standards
• Demonstrate a working knowledge of rules, regulations, and procedures of operating an automobile.
• Use visual search skills to obtain correct information and make reduced-risk decisions for effective speed and position adjustments.
• Interact with other users within the Highway Transportation System by adjusting speed, space, and communications to avoid conflicts and reduce risk.
• Demonstrate balanced vehicle movement through steering, braking, and accelerating in a precise and timely manner throughout a variety of adverse conditions.
Source: Goals from American Driver and Traffic Safety Education Association</td><td colspan="2">Students will be able to independently use their learning to…
• Drive courteously and defensively without accidents or needless risk.
• Adapt their knowledge of safe driving to various traffic, road, and weather conditions.</td></tr>
<tr><th colspan="2">Meaning</th></tr>
<tr><td>Understandings
Students will understand that…
• A motor vehicle can become a lethal weapon, and driving one demands constant attention.
• Defensive driving assumes that other drivers are inattentive and might make unexpected or dangerous moves.
• Effective drivers constantly adapt their driving to various traffic, road, and weather conditions.</td><td>Essential Questions
Students will keep considering…
• What must I anticipate and do to minimize risk and accidents when I drive?
• What makes a courteous and defensive driver?</td></tr>
<tr><th colspan="2">Acquisition</th></tr>
<tr><td>Students will know…
• Basic car parts and functions.
• Driving laws and rules of the road for their jurisdiction.
• Meaning of traffic signs and signals.
• What to do in case of an accident.</td><td>Students will be skilled at…
• Adjusting the driver's seat and car mirrors.
• Coordinating the gas and brake pedals.
• Signaling intentions.
• Merging into traffic on a highway.
• Parallel parking.</td></tr>
</table>

Source: Based on *The Understanding by Design Guide to Creating High-Quality Units* (pp. 18–20), by Grant Wiggins and Jay McTighe, 2011, Alexandria, VA: ASCD. Copyright 2011 by Grant Wiggins and Jay McTighe. Adapted with permission.

You saw in Figure 2.1 that Stage 2 of backward design contains three main categories: *Performance Tasks, Supplementary Evidence* (both under the umbrella of *Assessment Evidence*), and *Evaluative Criteria*. We believe that performance tasks are generally best suited to assess whether students understand important ideas and can transfer their learning to new situations. Indeed, an effective performance task sets up an authentic situation that calls for transfer.

The *Supplementary Evidence* section of the template offers a place to list other (often more traditional) assessments of knowledge, skill, and standards that are not otherwise assessed by the performance task. For example, if we want to see if students *know* state capitals or math facts, we might use a multiple-choice, matching, true-false, or fill-in-the-blank assessment format to efficiently provide the needed evidence. Similarly, we can assess for proficiency of individual *skills* by using a skill check or simple demonstration. In the driving example, teachers can use traditional tests to check students' knowledge of driving regulations and the meaning of traffic signs and signals.

Evaluative criteria are needed for performance tasks and any other open-ended assessments that do not have a single correct answer. These criteria, shown on the left side of the template, serve as the basis for assessing student performance. (Note: Identified criteria can be used to develop more detailed scoring rubrics as needed.)

Figure 2.3 displays a completed Stage 2 template for the driver education example. This example shows six performance tasks with associated criteria. Six is an appropriate number because this is an entire course and driving is a performance-based activity. (Most shorter curriculum units designed for academic subject matter would typically show one or two performance tasks.) The supplementary assessments include tests of knowledge and observations of particular skills because these are also listed goals in Stage 1 and should be assessed.

Stage 3 is where teachers develop the learning plan for a unit or course. Again, the logic of backward design reminds us that our learning plan needs to be tightly aligned with our goals (as identified in Stage 1) to help learners *acquire* targeted knowledge and skills, *make meaning* of important ideas, and be equipped to *transfer* their learning in meaningful ways. The learning plan should also prepare students for the corresponding assessments outlined in Stage 2.

Figure 2.3 Stage 2 of the UbD Unit Template with Driver Education Example

Stage 2—Evidence	
Evaluative Criteria	**Assessment Evidence**
• Skillful • Controlled • Defensive • Attentive • Courteous • Responsive • Accurate • Clear and complete explanation • Passed	**Performance Task(s)** *Task 1*: Drive to and from a designated location (e.g., from home to school and back) during daylight hours in light traffic to demonstrate skillful, responsive, courteous, and defensive driving under real-world conditions. *Task 2*: Same as Task #1 but in rainy conditions. *Task 3*: Same as Task #1 but in rush-hour traffic. *Task 4:* Same as Task #1 but after dark. *Task 5:* Study Guide: Develop a study guide of advice for beginning drivers to introduce and explain key understandings about safe and effective driving. *Task 6:* Road test required for obtaining a driver's license.
• Knowledgeable • Controlled • Skilled • Passed	**Supplementary Evidence** • Quiz on rules of the road and knowledge of signs and symbols. • Observation of student driver in a driving simulator or while practicing in car (off road). • Skill tests—backing up, parallel parking, merging into traffic. • Written test required for obtaining a driver's license.

Source: Based on *The Understanding by Design Guide to Creating High-Quality Units* (pp. 18–20), by Grant Wiggins and Jay McTighe, 2011, Alexandria, VA: ASCD. Copyright 2011 by Grant Wiggins and Jay McTighe. Adapted with permission.

Because a fundamental process of the brain involves linking new information to memory networks related to prior knowledge, teachers must find out what students already know (or think they know) before introducing a new topic. Accordingly, you'll note a section at the top of the Stage 3 section of the UbD template (see Figure 2.1) for identifying the *pre-assessments* that will be used to check students' prior knowledge (including possible misconceptions), skill levels, and interests related to the unit topic.

The Stage 3 template includes a separate column on the right side for planning the *formative assessments* that will be used to gauge learning along the way and to provide the feedback needed for adjustments. An extensive research base (Black & Wiliam, 1998; Hattie, 2008) reminds us that frequent, timely, and understandable feedback is one of the highest-yielding classroom strategies. Accordingly, we should include formative assessments in our learning plans—by design!

When drafting a unit, curriculum designers need not initially develop Stage 3 into full-blown lesson plans with all the details mapped out. The key in unit design is to see the bigger picture—to determine what learning experiences and instruction are needed, what resources will be used, and what sequence will optimize learning and student engagement. Once designers have developed a general outline, they can flesh out more detailed lesson plans as needed. Figure 2.4 presents a brief outline of the learning plan for the driver training course.

UbD Design Standards

Accompanying the UbD template is a set of design standards corresponding to each stage of backward design (see Figure 2.5). The standards offer criteria, framed as questions, for use during unit development and for quality control of completed unit designs. The UbD design standards serve curriculum designers in the same way that a scoring rubric serves students; teachers can periodically check to see, for example, if the identified understandings are truly big ideas or if the assessment evidence is properly aligned to the goals.

Teachers can also use these standards to guide peer reviews when they work collegially to examine their draft units and identify needed refinements *before* enacting them in the classroom. Our profession rarely subjects teacher-designed units and assessments to this level of critical

Figure 2.4 Stage 3 of the UbD Unit Template with Driver Education Example

Stage 3—Learning Plan	
Pre-assessment of driving knowledge and skills using a pre-test (nongraded) and driving simulators.	*Pre-assessment*
Learning Events *Note: The following provides a brief overview of a learning plan.* • Driving skills are developed and formatively assessed based on a four-level rubric distinguishing degrees of skill proficiency and autonomy: - The skill is introduced and modeled via video and the driving instructor. - The skill is practiced under instructor's direction in a controlled situation with instructor feedback. - The skill is practiced independently in a controlled situation with instructor feedback. - The skill is autonomously and effectively applied in varied situations (e.g., daylight, wet roads, nighttime, highway, city, country, rush hour). Car Check / Reversing Safety Checks / Parking Controls and Instruments / Emergency Stopping Starting, Moving, and Stopping / Anticipation and Planning Ahead Safe Positioning / Use of Speed Mirrors / Other Traffic Signals / Intersections Circles / Darkness Pedestrian Crossings / Weather Conditions Highways / Rules and Laws Turns • Student and instructor discuss the essential questions after each virtual and actual driving experience. • Students self-assess after each virtual and actual driving experience.	*Formative Assessments* Formative assessment and feedback by the instructor as students apply skills on the simulator and on the road. Instructor looks for common misconceptions and skill deficits, such as the following: • Failure to check mirrors and use peripheral vision. • Not adapting to changing road, weather, or traffic conditions. • Failure to give complete attention when driving. • Inaccurately judging the speed of oncoming cars during merges and turns. • Following other cars too closely.

Source: Based on *The Understanding by Design Guide to Creating High-Quality Units* (pp. 18–20), by Grant Wiggins and Jay McTighe, 2011, Alexandria, VA: ASCD. Copyright 2011 by Grant Wiggins and Jay McTighe. Adapted with permission.

Figure 2.5 UbD Design Standards

3 = Meets the standard; 2 = Partially meets the standard; 1 = Does not meet the standard.			
To what extent does the unit plan...			
Stage 1	**3**	**2**	**1**
1. Identify important, transferable ideas worth exploring and understanding?			
2. Identify understandings stated as full-sentence generalizations: *Students will understand that...?*			
3. Specify the desired long-term transfer goals that involve genuine accomplishment?			
4. Frame open-ended, thought-provoking, and focusing essential questions?			
5. Identify relevant standards, mission, or program goals to be addressed in all three stages?			
6. Identify knowledge and skills needed to achieve understanding and address the established goals?			
7. Align all the elements so that Stage 1 is focused and coherent?			
Stage 2			
8. Specify valid assessment evidence of all desired results; i.e., Stage 2 aligns with Stage 1?			
9. Include authentic performance tasks based on one or more facets of understanding?			
10. Provide sufficient opportunities for students to reveal their achievement?			
11. Include evaluative criteria to align each task to desired results and to provide suitable feedback on performance?			
Stage 3			
12. Include learning events and instruction needed to help learners—			
a. Acquire targeted knowledge and skills?			
b. Make meaning of important ideas?			
c. Transfer their learning to new situations?			
13. Effectively incorporate the WHERETO elements so that the unit is likely to be engaging and effective for all learners?*			
Overall			
14. Align all three stages as a coherent whole?			

*See Chapter 6 for information on WHERETO.

Source: *The Understanding by Design Guide to Creating High-Quality Units* (p. 27), by G. Wiggins and J. McTighe, 2011, Alexandria, VA: ASCD.

review. Nonetheless, we have found structured peer reviews, guided by the UbD design standards, to be enormously beneficial, and participants in peer review sessions regularly comment on the value of sharing and discussing curriculum and assessment designs with colleagues.

Chapter Understandings

- A primary goal of education is the development and deepening of student understanding of important ideas and processes in the disciplines.
- Evidence of student understanding is revealed when students apply (transfer) their learning within authentic contexts.
- Understanding must be "earned" by the learner. Teaching for understanding facilitates *meaning making* by the students and equips them to successfully transfer their learning.
- Effective curriculum development reflects a three-stage design process called *backward design*. This process helps to ensure that curriculum plans are well aligned and focused on desired learning. Backward curriculum design also helps avoid problems related to teaching that consists primarily of textbook coverage or is excessively activity oriented.
- Regular reviews of curriculum and assessment designs, based on design standards, are needed for quality control to avoid the most common design mistakes and disappointing results.
- Educators can "work smarter" in curriculum design by working collaboratively and sharing ideas via electronic networks.

Questions and Answers

Do you have to follow the UbD template order (top to bottom) when you design a unit?

No. Backward design does *not* demand a rigid sequence. The process of thinking through a unit design is inherently nonlinear and iterative, with various entry points. In fact, it is quite common that as teachers work through backward design, they return to adjust some aspect of Stage 1 as they work on the assessments in Stage 2 or the learning plan in Stage 3. However, the most important point is the final product—a coherent and aligned unit plan that is likely to engage students in authentic learning and collect evidence of the effect.

Can you use the three-stage UbD template for planning lessons as well as units?

We have chosen the unit as a focus for design because the key elements of UbD—coming to understand important ideas, consider essential questions, and engage in performances of transfer—are too complex and multifaceted to be satisfactorily addressed within a single lesson.

Nonetheless, the larger unit goals provide the context in which purposeful and focused individual lessons are planned. In fact, teachers often report that the careful attention they give to curriculum planning in Stages 1 and 2 sharpens their lesson planning, resulting in more purposeful teaching and improved learning.

3

Goals: The Drivers of Everything

The brain learns most efficiently and effectively when it is motivated by worthy and desirable goals. In this chapter, we'll consider learning goals from two perspectives: (1) goals to guide schools and teachers, and (2) goals that focus and motivate students. We'll examine each of these perspectives and offer specific examples and practical techniques to address them.

Learning Goals for the Modern World

Today's students will need to navigate vastly different sources, varieties, and quantities of information to meet the more complex demands of our new information and economic landscapes. Consider how many jobs from the past decades do not exist today (e.g., one-hour photo developing, pumping gas, repairing cassette and videotape machines, reading utility meters). Similarly, think about how many of today's jobs did not exist 20 years ago (e.g., manufacturing and installation of solar panels and wind turbines, developing apps for smartphones and tablets, online customer service and support, programming robots for manufacturing). This trend of new—and unpredictable—career opportunities is likely to continue and accelerate, while the skill sets required by many of these jobs will become increasingly sophisticated.

The National Association of Colleges and Employers (NACE) conducts an annual survey of employers to gather data about what they look for when hiring new college graduates. (See www.naceweb.org/s11182015/employers-look-for-in-new-hires.aspx.) Here are the summarized results of its 2016 Job Outlook survey, showing a rank ordering of the desired job qualities and skills as reported by employers (NACE, 2016).

Leadership	80.1%
Ability to work in a team	78.9%
Communication skills (written)	70.2%
Problem-solving skills	70.2%
Communication skills (verbal)	68.9%
Strong work ethic	68.9%
Initiative	65.8%
Analytical/quantitative skills	62.7%
Flexibility/adaptability	60.9%
Technical skills	59.6%
Interpersonal skills (relates well to others)	58.4%
Computer skills	55.3%
Detail oriented	52.8%
Organizational ability	48.4%
Friendly/outgoing personality	35.4%
Strategic planning skills	26.7%
Creativity	23.6%
Tactfulness	20.5%
Entrepreneurial skills/risk-taker	18.6%

Notice that most of these qualities and skills require executive functions!

In acknowledging the nature of the skill sets needed in the modern workplace, Linda Darling-Hammond, a professor at Stanford University and an authority on international assessments, suggests implications for education:

> As educators, we know that today's students will enter a workforce in which they will have to not only acquire information, but also analyze, synthesize, and apply it to address new problems, design solutions, collaborate effectively, and communicate persuasively. Few, if any, previous generations have been asked to become such nimble thinkers. (Darling-Hammond & Adamson, 2013, p. 1)

To summarize, if students leave school without the executive function skill sets that develop during the critical years when the brain's prefrontal cortex is maturing, their preparation for the world's challenges and opportunities will be substantially inadequate.

By making these employment-related points, we are not implying that the sole purpose of an education is job preparation. Certainly, outcomes such as responsible citizenship and lifelong wellness are desirable goals of schooling. However, as parents of millennials, we are mindful of the need for young people to develop the skills needed for gainful and satisfying employment as one dimension of a fulfilling life. No one is happy when 20-somethings are stuck living in their parents' basements because they are unqualified for available jobs!

Establishing Curricular Goals

Just as individual brains are goal directed, educators need learning goals to help direct and focus their efforts. Research has confirmed that teacher clarity about what they want their students to learn is one of the most significant factors related to student achievement (Hattie, 2008; Marzano, 1998). In his book *Clarity in the Classroom,* New Zealand educator Michael Absolum (2006) highlights the importance of task clarity and summarizes the benefits:

> For students to truly be able to take responsibility for their learning, both teachers and students need to be very clear about what is being learned, and how they should go about it. When learning and the path toward it are clear, research shows that there are a number of important shifts for students. Their motivation improves, they stay on task, their behavior improves and they are able to take more responsibility for their learning. (p. 76)

From a curriculum design perspective, goal clarity is the critical starting point of UbD because everything, including learning experiences, instructional resources, assessments, and schedule, should be planned *backward* from the targeted goals. One dimension of goal clarity is the recognition that there are different kinds of learning goals. The differences matter, in terms of both how teachers teach for different goals and how each is most appropriately assessed. The following sections describe different types of goals.

Goals Related to Knowledge

Knowledge goals specify what students should know. This category focuses on declarative knowledge of factual information (e.g., multiplication tables, state capitals), vocabulary terms, and basic concepts (e.g., *interdependence, adaptation*). From an instructional standpoint, teachers can impart factual knowledge through a lecture or by having learners read informational texts. (In Chapter 5, we'll explore a number of brain-friendly techniques for enhancing memory storage and retrieval of factual knowledge.) As for assessment, teachers can gauge the attainment of knowledge goals through questioning and by using objective test and quiz items.

Goals Related to Skills and Processes

Goals for skills and processes are procedural in nature; they state what students should be able to *do*. Some skills involve relatively simple behaviors, such as tying a knot or adding numbers. Others, such as writing an essay or conducting a scientific investigation, are actually more complex processes involving a number of specific skills working together. Skill proficiency is best developed through an instructional process involving modeling, guided practice, and feedback. Teachers assess student proficiency in a skill or process through direct observation of a performance, as might occur in physical education; or by examining a product, such as a piece of writing. Unlike assessment of knowledge, which usually looks for a single "correct" answer, the assessment of skills and processes can best be conceived as a continuum of proficiency levels from novice to expert—similar to the different colored belts used in karate.

Goals Related to Understanding

Goals for understanding refer to the *big ideas* that we want students to comprehend at a deep level. Such ideas are inherently conceptual and abstract. They may be in the form of concepts (e.g., *migration*), principles (e.g., *F=MA*), themes (e.g., *friendship*), or processes (e.g., *problem solving*). In UbD, desired understandings are stated as full-sentence generalizations (e.g., *A muscle that contracts through its full range of motion will generate more force*).

Teaching for understanding requires more than simple didactic presentation and rote learning. Teachers must facilitate *meaning making* by the learner, using instructional methods such as Socratic questioning, concept attainment, inquiry, and problem-based learning. It is precisely this way of teaching that yields a dual benefit: (1) deepening of subject matter understanding and (2) strengthening the brain's neural networks associated with its executive functions.

The most appropriate assessments of understanding are not multiple-choice or fill-in-the-blank test items. Understanding is evident when students can effectively do two things: (1) *apply* their learning to a new situation—that is, transfer; and (2) *explain* their thinking to justify their conclusion or answer. Thus we recommend using performance-based assessments and rubrics to gauge the degree of a student's understanding. (We will explore assessing understanding and transfer in more detail in Chapter 4.)

We have found it helpful to frame desired understandings through *essential questions*, and you can think of understandings and essential questions as two sides of a coin. Although essential questions are not goals, per se, they can help to clarify desired understandings, spark student inquiry, and engage higher-order thinking. Figure 3.1 shows examples of related understandings and essential questions for academic subject areas.

Goals Related to Transfer

A fourth goal type involves transfer. Transfer refers to students' capacity to apply what they have learned to a new situation, beyond the context in which it was learned. Transfer goals specify what we want students to *be able to do with their learning* in the long run when confronted by new opportunities and challenges. In a world in which people can access much of the world's knowledge on a smartphone, it is no longer enough for educators to simply prepare learners to give back existing knowledge. A modern education should equip learners to use executive functions to apply their learning to address new—even unpredictable—opportunities and challenges, within and outside school. In other words, school must develop *know-how*, not just knowledge.

In *Education for Life and Work: Developing Transferable Knowledge and Skills in the 21st Century*, the National Research Council (2012) characterizes transfer goals as the essence of 21st century learning:

> We define "deeper learning" as the process through which an individual becomes capable of taking what was learned in one situation and applying it to new situations (i.e., transfer). Through deeper learning (which often involves shared learning

and interactions with others in a community), the individual develops expertise in a particular domain of knowledge and/or performance.... The product of deeper learning is transferable knowledge, including content knowledge in a domain and knowledge of how, why, and when to apply this knowledge to answer questions and solve problems. We refer to this blend of both knowledge and skills as "21st century competencies." (p. 6)

Figure 3.1 Sample Understandings and Essential Questions for Academic Subjects

Understandings	Essential Questions
Effective readers actively monitor their comprehension to ensure they understand what they are reading.	• *What do good readers do?* • *How will I know that I understand what I am reading?*
A muscle that contracts through its full range of motion will generate more force.	• *How can I hit* [e.g., a golf ball, tennis ball, or baseball] *with greater power without losing control?*
Visual artists choose to follow or break established conventions in pursuit of expressive goals.	• *Why and when should an artist depart from established conventions?*
Statistical analysis and data display can reveal patterns that may not be obvious. Pattern recognition enables prediction.	• *Is there a pattern here?* • *What will/might happen next?*
Language is embedded within a cultural context, and acquisition requires much more than word-for-word translation.	• *Why isn't a dictionary enough (when learning to speak a new language)?*
Scientific claims must be verified by independent investigations and replications.	• *How do I know what to believe about a scientific claim?* • *When and how do scientific conjectures become facts?*
Measure twice, cut once.	• *How can I avoid costly errors?*
Audience and purpose influence a writer's choice of organizational pattern, language, and literary techniques to elicit an intended response from the reader.	• *Why am I writing? What is my purpose?* • *Who is my audience? What will work best for my audience?*

The Latin origin of the term *curriculum* translates roughly as "the course to be run," and it is useful to think of a curriculum as the course or pathway to a destination. Our contention is that long-term transfer goals—both within and across academic disciplines—reflect *the* destination of a contemporary K–12 education. Accordingly, we should plan the curriculum backward from these important outcomes.

Practically speaking, we are *not* suggesting that every teacher should come up with her own list of transfer goals for every unit she teaches. Instead, we propose that district- and school-level curriculum teams identify a set of transfer goals as long-term exit outcomes—goals to be attained by the end of a K–12 education. Such goals bring specificity to the phrase "college- and career-ready." We further recommend that there be only a small number of truly long-term transfer goals for each discipline and a small number that cut across the disciplines. For example, a long-term transfer goal in history is for students to reference the lessons of the past when they consider contemporary issues, whereas a transfer goal in mathematics is for students to be able to use sound mathematical reasoning and strategies to tackle real-world problems. Cross-disciplinary transfer goals include those requiring the brain's executive functions, such as *critical thinking*, *collaboration*, and *creativity*. Figure 3.2 presents examples of long-term transfer goals within academic disciplines.

Cross-Disciplinary Transfer Goals for Executive Functions

Another category of transfer goals cuts across the disciplines and is associated with the executive functions of the brain. We contend that teachers can enhance academic learning while *concurrently* developing these mental processes. This means that educators should specify what they want students to come to understand about their brain and its controls, pose essential questions to help develop those understandings, and remind students to invoke them when needed. Figure 3.3 presents examples of understandings about various executive functions and associated essential questions that may be used to develop these lifelong capacities.

Clarity about long-term transfer goals, within and across the disciplines, helps teachers and students truly keep the "end in mind." These goals help teachers prioritize and focus their teaching and avoid getting lost in the weeds of trying to "cover" long lists of discrete facts and skills. For students, transfer goals speak to relevance because they identify ways to apply learning to real-life situations.

Teaching for transfer means equipping learners to apply their learning to a *new* and specific setting in which sensitivity to context matters. We hope it is evident that the development of long-term transfer capacities requires use of the brain's executive functions. Rote learning from lectures can never prepare students for such outcomes (Wiggins & McTighe, 2011).

Figure 3.2 Examples of Long-Term Transfer Goals Within Academic Disciplines
Students will be able to independently use their learning to...
Economics Make economically sound and ethical financial decisions.
History Use knowledge of patterns of history to help understand the present and prepare for the future.
Health and Physical Education Make healthful choices and decisions throughout their lives.
Mathematics Apply sound mathematical reasoning and strategies to tackle real-world problems.
Reading Comprehend texts in various genres (literature, nonfiction, technical) for various purposes (e.g., for entertainment, to be informed, to perform a task).
Research Locate pertinent information from varied sources (print, online; primary, secondary).
Science Conduct a sound investigation to answer an empirical question.
World Language Effectively communicate with varied audiences and for varied purposes while displaying appropriate cultural understanding.
Writing Write in various genres for various purposes and audiences.

Goals in the UbD Template

When using the UbD framework for curriculum planning and design, educators should "unpack" standards- and mission-related

Figure 3.3 Sample Understandings and Essential Questions for the Brain's Executive Functions

Understandings	Essential Questions
Attention Focus Optimal learning requires the ability to selectively focus the brain's attention to prioritize the most important sensory data/information while blocking distracting/irrelevant input.	• *What should I focus on?* • *What strategies can I use to focus my attention and resist distractions?*
Goal Setting Effective learners set specific, measurable goals and make plans to achieve them, monitor their progress toward goal achievement, and make needed adjustments in response to feedback or new information. Goal-oriented people resist immediate gratification in order to work toward future goals.	• *What is my goal or desired outcome?* • *What steps are needed to achieve this goal?* • *What obstacle(s) might impede my progress?* • *How can I obtain helpful feedback?* • *What can I learn from setbacks or mistakes?* • *What adjustments are needed?* • *How might I delay my desire for immediate gratification in order to achieve a long-term goal?*
Prioritizing Prioritizing involves determining hierarchies of importance and managing time and resources effectively in order to achieve the most important goals.	• *What is most important here?* • *What should I do first? Second?* • *What action will be most effective? Least effective?* • *What is the best use of my time and resources?*
Critical Thinking Critical thinkers do not simply believe whatever they read, hear, or view. They remain skeptical, ask critical questions, and seek alternative points of view before reaching decisions or taking actions.	• *How do I know what to believe in what I read, hear, and view? Just what is true?* • *What other perspectives should I consider?*
Decision Making One's choices and actions have consequences. Effective decision making requires judgment regarding possible choices/actions and associated outcomes, risks, and consequences. Specific criteria are needed to evaluate options and guide decisions.	• *How should I decide?* • *By what criteria will I evaluate options and guide decisions?* • *What are possible consequences of my choices or actions?*
Cognitive Flexibility An intellectually mature person looks for varied ways of defining problems, considers different points of view, tries alternative strategies/approaches, and explores new solutions and possibilities.	• *In what other ways might I define this problem?* • *Are there other ways of viewing this situation?* • *What can I do when my approach is not working?* • *What are other possibilities and solutions?* • *When should I "shift gears" and try a new approach?*

Understandings	Essential Questions
Delaying Gratification Resisting a smaller but more immediate reward can enable one to achieve a larger or more enduring reward later. Instead of acting or responding immediately to temptations, effective people exert self-control and consider the short- and long-term impacts of their actions.	• *Why can't I just have what I want when I want it?* • *How can I avoid temptations that may distract me from my long-term goal(s)?* • *How can I control myself?*
Metacognitive Self-management Capacity for metacognitive self-management includes active and ongoing monitoring of one's cognitive and emotional states and making needed adjustments based on insights in response to feedback and new information. Effective learners reflect on their experiences and learn from them.	• *How am I doing?* • *How can I monitor my cognitive and emotional states?* • *What are my strengths and weaknesses?* • *How can I obtain helpful feedback?* • *What adjustments are needed?* • *What did I learn from this experience?*

outcomes by considering each of these goal types—knowledge, skills, understandings, and transfer. Figure 3.4 presents the UbD Unit Design Template for Stage 1, with its associated planning questions shown under Transfer (for transfer goals), Meaning (for goals related to understandings), and Acquisition (for goals related to knowledge and skills).

Goal Setting for and by Students

We now consider learning goals from the viewpoint of the learner. The brain learns with maximum efficiency when it is motivated by desirable goals, and students will be more likely to focus their efforts and persist in learning when

- The learning goals are clear.
- They see the goals as having personal relevance and value.
- They know how their achievement will be recognized (e.g., via known tasks and success criteria).
- They believe that the goals are attainable and they can see their progress toward achieving the goals.

Let's consider each of these factors, along with practical techniques for addressing them.

Figure 3.4 UbD Unit Design Template for Stage 1

<table>
<tr><th colspan="3">Stage 1—Desired Results</th></tr>
<tr><td rowspan="6">Established Goals
What content standards and program- or mission-related goal(s) will this unit address?

What habits of mind and cross-disciplinary goal(s)—for example, 21st century skills, core competencies—will this unit address?</td><td colspan="2">Transfer</td></tr>
<tr><td colspan="2">Students will be able to independently use their learning to . . .

What kinds of long-term independent accomplishments are desired?</td></tr>
<tr><td colspan="2">Meaning</td></tr>
<tr><td>UNDERSTANDINGS
Students will understand that . . .

What specifically do you want students to understand?

What inferences should they make?</td><td>ESSENTIAL QUESTIONS
Students will keep considering . . .

What thought-provoking questions will foster inquiry, meaning-making, and transfer?</td></tr>
<tr><td colspan="2">Acquisition</td></tr>
<tr><td>Students will know . . .

What facts and basic concepts should students know and be able to recall?</td><td>Students will be skilled at . . .

What discrete skills and processes should students be able to use?</td></tr>
</table>

Source: From *The Understanding by Design Guide to Creating High-Quality Units* (p. 16), by G. Wiggins and J. McTighe (2011), Alexandria, VA: ASCD. Copyright © 2011 by Grant Wiggins and Jay McTighe. Adapted with permission.

Goal Clarity

Learners are more likely to focus their efforts when the learning goal is clear and they see it as worthwhile. Clarity in goal planning is needed to prime the pleasure-seeking brain to invest the effort to achieve a clear goal. It is therefore essential to be clear from the start as to what the goals of the learning will be and to communicate these goals early to students. Neuroscience studies confirm that goal clarity positively affects students' motivation and their capacity to organize and focus their efforts, leading to enhanced academic performance. The process begins with clear teaching goals and is enhanced when students participate in setting their own goals (Morisano et al., 2010; Prabhakar et al., 2016). Conversely, when the goal is unclear or irrelevant to students, it is unlikely that they will maintain attention, try their best, or persist when learning becomes challenging.

If curriculum planners have done well in their Stage 1 efforts, the various learning goals they want learners to attain (transfer, understandings, knowledge, and skills) should be crystal clear. The next step is to bring that clarity to the learners. Teachers can take a number of practical actions in this regard, including the following:

- Directly state the desired goals/outcomes at the beginning of a new unit. Then, connect daily lesson goals to the longer-term unit goals.
- Post and discuss the essential questions at the start of the unit and refer to them throughout.
- Invite student questions about the unit topic and allow students to explore them. Using KWL charts at the beginning of a unit can increase students' goal ownership because they can pose questions and identify those aspects of a subject about which they are curious and *W*ant to learn. (Note: The KWL strategy also activates students' prior knowledge by asking them what they already ***K***now. Additionally, if students create their own individual KWL charts, they can incorporate their own goals—things they particularly want to know that are relevant to the coming unit of study. They will see their progress toward their personal goal as the unit continues, and they can fill in the chart sections about what they have *L*earned and make corrections to any errors in the K column.)

- Present the ways in which students can demonstrate their learning—the assessments—and discuss the associated success criteria. For example, in addition to traditional tests, students may be asked to plan a lesson for kids in a lower grade. Knowing in advance they will teach a concept to younger children motivates students to put more effort into learning a concept fully and keeps their minds focused when they practice.
- Share samples of work from previous years' students that illustrate the desired learning. Tangible examples make the goals and assessment criteria come to life.

Goal Relevance and Value

Goal clarity is necessary but insufficient on its own. Brains are goal-driven, but only if the goal is seen as personally relevant and having some value. As adults, how many of us will put forth maximum effort to learn something new that we do not care about or that we think we will never use? Accepting a goal as relevant and valuable, or worthwhile, is especially important to school-age learners who may not always see inherent value in what they are being asked to learn. Indeed, it is not uncommon to encounter questions such as "Why are we learning this?" or "Whoever uses this stuff?" from skeptical students. Without believable answers, how can we expect learners to commit a whole-hearted effort to learning? Accordingly, teachers need to plan assiduously to help students see relevance in, and make personal connections to, targeted learning goals. Here are several practical techniques for promoting student acceptance of goals:

- Demonstrate or discuss the "so what?" factor. Identify people and places beyond the classroom where the knowledge and skills are applied.
- Watch a relevant video to help students see real-world value in what they are being asked to learn. Two good sources are PBS Learning Media (www.pbslearningmedia.org) and the Futures Channel (www.thefutureschannel.com).
- Describe how students will be able to use their new learning during or after achieving the goals, such as through a project or performance task, teaching younger students, or presenting to an authentic audience. Using authentic performance tasks can make

learning more relevant and memorable while supporting conceptual understanding and the construction of enduring memory circuits.

- Use a "hook" question to engage learners in seeing the worthiness and relevance of a goal. For example, a 7th grade health teacher begins a unit on nutrition with the question "How can what you eat help prevent zits?" to help her students recognize the personal benefits of learning the designated content.
- Spark acceptance by "selling" the parts of the unit that you know will be particularly engaging. For example, as part of a mathematics unit involving percent and decimals, describe how the unit will be taught through a simulation of personal banking in which students will have blank checks, a check register, deposit slips, and choices of transactions (e.g., purchases from shopping catalogs or investments) for them to do with the "money" in their accounts.
- Invite students to tell personal stories of how the topic relates to their lives, or ask them to brainstorm how they might be able to apply the new learning both now and in the future.
- Before a lesson or unit, tell an anecdote about the life of the author, scientist, historical figure, or mathematician when that individual was about the age of your students.

When planning sections of units that students may not recognize as intrinsically interesting or clearly linked to personally desirable goals, teachers can use the brain's natural curiosity to boost students' interest and engagement. Neurologically, curiosity and prediction activate the brain's dopamine-reward system to fuel attention and sustained effort.

One way to engage students' curiosity is to emulate certain techniques used by advertisers to gain the attention and interest of their audience. For example, the "coming attractions" at a movie theater are meant to leave the viewer wanting more. The trailers are usually edited to be particularly dramatic and attention grabbing; they provide some indication of what the film is about but leave out most of the details. This technique creates suspense. The viewer, if successfully enticed, wants to see the full-length movie to see how things resolve.

Teachers can similarly "advertise" an upcoming unit to provoke curiosity about what's to come using a variety of low- and high-tech techniques. For example, cut up a picture of a poster, painting, or photograph relating to the content, and every day or so add pieces or clues leading up to a "big-idea understanding" about the topic. For fractions, these clues could include a picture of an x-ray of an arm fracture; sheet music with half, whole, and quarter notes; a carrot cut into quarters; a ball floating in water with part of it submerged; and a photo of an iceberg showing the proportions above and below water.

Here are other time-honored ways of sparking curiosity in the classroom:

- Present "weird facts" or discrepant events. For example, punch a balloon with a wooden skewer and ask students to speculate why the balloon did not burst.
- Show thought-provoking pictures, such as an M. C. Escher drawing, or short video clips, such as the opening scenes of Ken Burns's documentary film *The Civil War*, depicting the horrors and personal impact of war.
- Use humor to open the door to a new topic. For example, show cartoons featuring exaggerated proportions to start a unit on ratio and proportion; tell a humorous anecdote about the misuse of vocabulary in a world language class.

Curiosity may fade, but the brain's permanent wiring dictates the need to find out if a prediction is correct. Recall the dopamine-reward response described in Chapter 1. A correct prediction can trigger this response, leading the brain to correct faulty knowledge from incorrect predictions and to reward successful predictions and responses or choices. Just as curiosity engages attention, prediction sustains attention because the brain *wants* to know if its predictions are correct. (Think of adults who pick a favorite in a horse race and then judiciously watch the race to see if they hold a winning ticket.) Teachers can use the brain's need to validate predictions. After hooking learners with various attention-getters, teachers can sustain their attention by asking them to predict what they think the curiosity-stimulating sight, sound, object, statement, picture, or question might have to do with the lesson.

It is important that all students make predictions, using either low-tech methods, such as "thumbs up, thumbs down" or writing on individual whiteboards or "magic pads," or through high-tech devices, such as student-response clickers or smartphone apps. Because students can change their predictions, their brains sustain buy-in because they want to know what you have to teach!

Recognizing Goal Achievement

When students are aware of the criteria by which educational goals will be assessed, they show better long-term academic development than do their peers who are focused only on a final grade or are motivated by outperforming others. By knowing the criteria in advance, students are provided with clear expectations regarding the quality of their work. There is no mystery as to the desired elements of quality or the basis for evaluation and grading. Students don't have to guess about what is most important or how their achievement will be judged.

Teachers can use a number of practical techniques to help learners understand how their achievement will be recognized. Here are some examples:

- Present success criteria at the start of a new unit.
- Involve students in identifying preliminary evaluation criteria.
- Show models/exemplars for expected products/performances.
- Have students review examples and induce the characteristics of the most effective ones.
- Show and explain scoring rubrics to clarify how students' work will be judged.

Attainability and Awareness of Progress Toward Goals

Learners benefit not only from knowing the learning goals and associated success criteria; they are more likely to persist on challenging tasks when they believe that the goals are *attainable* and that they are *making progress* toward those goals. Recall that the prefrontal cortex, where the goal-planning executive functions develop, is the last part of the brain to mature—a process that continues well into the 20s. Although it may seem obvious to adults, young people do not automatically recognize the correlation between their effort and goal attainment. For students to sustain effort on the way to reaching long-term goals, they need explicit feedback about, and affirmation of, their incremental progress. Providing recognition (and celebration) of goal progress can counteract the ingrained tendency for immediate gratification that is characteristic of the developing brains of school-age children and adolescents. As the video game model illustrates, the dopamine-reward response in the brain fuels a player's sustained effort—even through increasing challenges and setbacks.

Teachers can harness this effect by providing ongoing feedback on progress to promote students' persistence and reward sustained effort on important learning tasks. Here are practical techniques for promoting students' awareness of their progress toward worthy goals:

- Guide students in breaking down a long-term goal into a series of simpler goals that will build, step-by-step, toward the final goal. For example, if students are expected to read a 50-page book in two weeks, have them write down the five pages they'll read on each of 10 days and record each accomplishment. If a goal is to learn 25 new vocabulary words, create a "thermometer" graph and mark off progress points achieved along the way to that goal. These simple actions give the brain visual feedback and help learners experience the dopamine pleasure of recognizing tangible progress toward a goal.
- Model self-assessment using the success criteria and developed rubrics. Provide feedback on the accuracy of the students' own self-assessments.
- Guide students in using rubrics to identify where they are and where they need to go next for each trait or performance level.
- Involve students in identifying success criteria and have them develop their own individualized rubrics, using your general rubric.
- Use "effort-to-goal progress graphs" to keep track of incremental progress. These graphs are a type of visual organizer that students can use to keep progress records and create associated bar graphs, such as for time spent on practice, scores on quizzes, or feedback from teachers or peers (see www.onlinecharttool.com). For example, the graph shown in Figure 3.5 was developed by an 11th grade student whose goal was to improve his free-throw shooting in basketball. At each practice session, he took 25 shots and recorded the number of baskets he made. He also recorded the cumulative time he had put into practicing; that is, he added the time spent on each day's practice to the total time he had practiced thus far.

A visual model like that shown in Figure 3.5 allows students to see that their level of success is under their control. The graph provides visible evidence that greater *effort* (in this case, time spent practicing free throws) results in measurable *progress* toward a goal (an increasing percentage of successful free-throw shots). Because the measurements on the graph relate the progress toward a goal, students can savor successes without having to be embarrassed by their specific scores or the point of mastery to which they have progressed. The first designation on each student's graph simply indicates the individual "starting place," and subsequent points on the graph delineate the amounts by which the student increased or improved from that point.

Figure 3.5 Effort-to-Goal Progress Graph

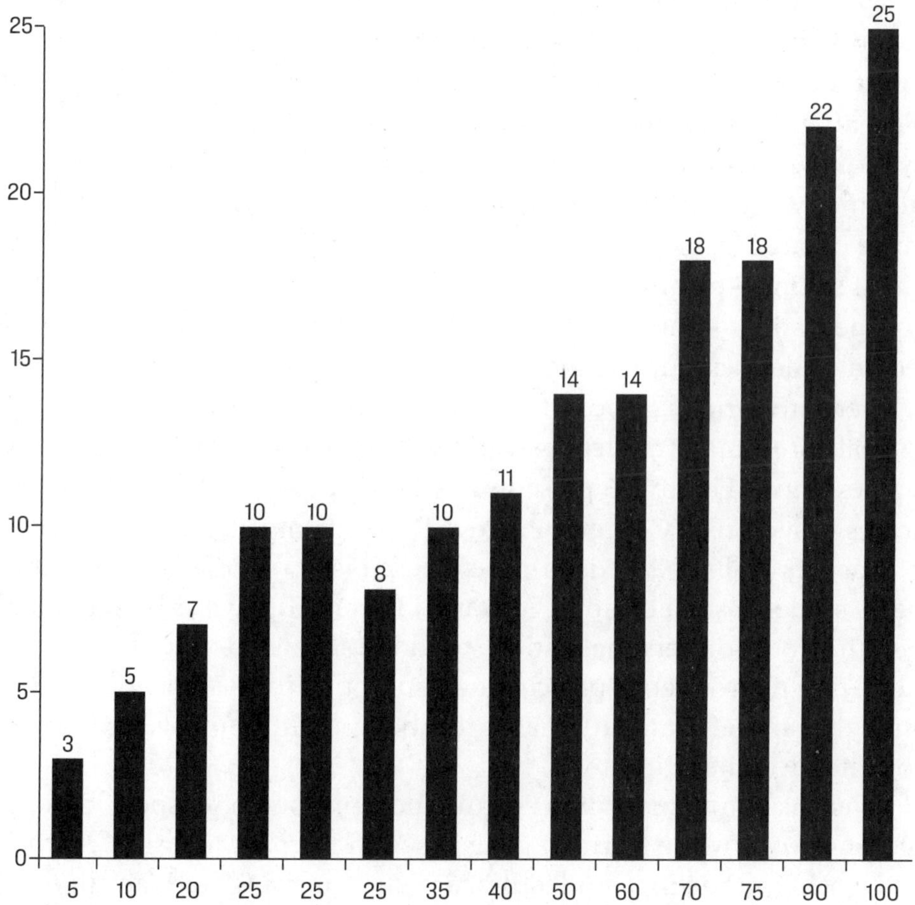

x = cumulative time practicing
y = number of baskets made

Record-keeping methods like this chart enable learners to track their progress and celebrate personal growth toward worthy learning goals. Recall that the brain's response to the awareness that it has achieved success releases a spike in dopamine, a neurochemical producing feelings of deep pleasure and satisfaction. When students recognize the association between progress toward (and achievement of) goals and the brain's reward response, they will be able to use their own internal motivation systems to sustain progress toward a goal.

Guiding Students in Personal Goal Setting

The educational goals referenced in this chapter thus far are identified by national or state standards or specified by teachers. However, educational goal setting can also be personalized. Teachers who guide their students in setting clear, achievable, and personally desirable goals reflect an understanding of how the brain learns best. When learners have some input into (or choices within) the learning process, they are often motivated to put forth greater effort, resulting in enhanced performance on academic tasks. Moreover, by engaging the skill sets involved in goal setting—prioritizing, planning, self-monitoring, seeking feedback, persisting—learners are strengthening the neural networks associated with these executive functions.

There are various options for allowing students to set personal learning goals or to make choices within the framework of established ones. As an example, Figure 3.6 presents a simple frame for allowing student choices based on a "Content, Process, Product" organizer.

Teachers will need to determine when it is appropriate and feasible to give students such options. Although it may not always be possible to open the door for personalization, we do not want to lose sight of the underlying neuroscience principle: whenever learners see a goal as personally meaningful and attainable for them, their brains will be more motivated to pursue it!

Of course, students will need guidance on how to set specific, achievable, and worthwhile learning goals. As with learning any skill, learners need teacher modeling, guided practice, and ongoing feedback in order to build the needed capacities. We have found it valuable to help students become aware of the basic neuroscience behind what makes their brains want to put forth effort to achieve goals. A teacher can explain how a big part of successful goal setting is related to the brain's inborn programming to try things when it believes there is something it wants and can achieve—with planning and effort. For example, a teacher might say, "Your brain is more likely to engage and be more responsive when it knows how you will benefit from any activity. Setting your own goals increases your brain's desire to achieve them. The more specifically you define your goal and acknowledge its value to you, the more effort your brain will put into achieving it."

Figure 3.6 Personal Goal Setting for Content, Process, and Product

Content: Students set personal goals related to the content outcomes.

Examples:

- Students in a history class studying World War II may be allowed to pursue personal interests. For instance, a student interested in aviation learns about various warplanes, whereas another student researches a famous person of the era, such as Anne Frank or Douglas MacArthur.
- Elementary students generate their own "I really want to know" questions related to a new topic. They have time to pursue their personal inquiries with assistance from the school librarian.

Process: Students set goals related to their learning process and make choices about the strategies that will be most effective for them.

Examples:

- A language learner may use podcasts to learn vocabulary, whereas another student chooses to practice with flashcards.
- Students choose personal techniques for note taking and studying, such as a traditional outline, graphic organizers, or summary note cards.

Product: Students set personal goals related to the products by which they will show their learning.

Examples:

- One student creates a visual "concept map" to show her understanding of cell structures and functions; another student writes a simulated textbook section for younger students.
- Middle school students working on an authentic performance task can pick from a list of product options, including a newspaper article, a presentation, a poster, a podcast, a graphic organizer, and a museum display.

Here are other practical actions that teachers can take to support students as they plan and monitor their learning goals.

- Model your own planning processes by thinking aloud about how you identify your own personal goals and how you make a specific plan to attain them.

- Just as you use students' interests, strengths, and talents to engage them in the goals you have developed, encourage them to recognize and use this information to set personalized goals.
- Provide opportunities for students to review weekly charts showing progress toward goal achievement and note which strategies were most effective for them.
- Teach students how to make schedules and manage time when planning long-term projects.
- Provide (or guide the construction of) goal-setting and self-monitoring tools, such as to-do lists, step-by-step guides, personalized rubrics, graphic organizers, and self-assessment prompts.
- Guide students in identifying personalized success criteria for self-assessing their achievement of targeted goals.
- Schedule brief "touch base" conferences with students to check in on their progress toward their goals.

As students become more experienced at setting personal goals based on their interests, strengths, and talents, they build their self-confidence as learners. When they choose learning and self-monitoring strategies that work for them, they develop greater autonomy and capacity for independent learning. With each success, the increased sense of their own competence will encourage them to confidently set and pursue higher goals, while also building the persistence, resilience, and greater tolerance needed to face inevitable setbacks.

Delaying Gratification

One of the brain's most critical executive functions is the ability to delay gratification, especially when working toward goals that are not immediate or tangible. This is a formidable habit of mind that undergirds the perseverance needed to achieve a long-term goal and sustains successful people through challenging times.

We propose that the concept of delayed gratification be introduced to younger students and reinforced throughout the grades. Teachers can explain the related neuroscience in developmentally appropriate ways. For example, help students understand that working toward worthwhile, long-term goals actually goes against their brain's programming. Developing brains are wired to favor immediate gratification, so they need to build the executive function skill sets in order to delay that drive and reap achievement rewards in the future.

Here are practical actions that teachers can take to develop students' capacities for delaying gratification in pursuit of worthy goals:

- Tell students stories that illustrate delayed gratification; cite characters in literature (e.g., *The Little Red Hen*) or real people (e.g., athletes) who have set long-term goals and made sacrifices in the short term to achieve them.
- Provide personal examples of times when you delayed gratification. Reveal how hard it was to resist temptation, explain how you kept at it, and relate the benefits that you realized through persistence.
- Have students share their own stories of successful delay of gratification.
- Use think-alouds to illustrate ways that you defer gratification, such as avoiding a sugary afternoon snack before a nutritious dinner.
- Use and revisit engaging and student-relevant essential questions throughout a unit. Remind students that their understanding will deepen as they consider and reconsider these open-ended questions.
- Teach students specific strategies that they can use to focus on long term goals—for example, writing down a long-term goal and then creating and posting an image or picture of the desired goal on a bulletin board.
- Model specific strategies students can use to delay immediate gratification, such as keeping progress charts, developing and following a study/practice schedule, and working with a learning buddy or study group.
- Post a list of basic "Delaying Gratification" strategies in the classroom. Add to the list throughout the year.
- Use metacognitive prompts such as these:
  - *What will I be able to do, understand, or create when I have achieved my goal(s)?*
  - *How might I avoid known distractions (e.g., social media, television, games, parties)?*
  - *How can I stay on track (e.g., daily check-in with a partner with a similar goal)?*

- Look for opportunities to highlight and celebrate occasions when students delayed gratification and achieved something in the long run.

As students develop their understanding about the benefits of, and strategies for, delaying gratification, they will become increasingly able to apply effort even when the pleasure of attaining a goal is not instantaneous. As they recognize the value of goal setting, practice, and application of learning, they will become better able to persist in working toward targeted goals—including the "boring" fundamentals and the very challenging topics.

Chapter Understandings

- Even as the prefrontal cortex of the brain develops during the school years, the goal-directed executive functions such as prioritizing, systematic planning, self-monitoring, and deferring gratification do not automatically emerge. Students need ongoing opportunities to develop these critical skills—and the neural networks that underpin them.
- With regular opportunities to set personal goals, learn and apply effective strategies, track their progress, and celebrate achievements, students will become increasingly able to transfer these goal-setting skills to other applications in school and life. Increasing goal-directed executive functions leads to greater persistence and enhanced self-control of attention focus, inhibition of distraction, and self-regulation.
- Given the intrinsic satisfaction of achieving a goal, students will be motivated to take on new challenges and persevere in working to attain them (Karakowsky & Mann, 2008; Prabhakar et al., 2016).
- There are qualitatively different types of educational goals, including Knowledge, Skills, Understandings, and long-term Transfer Goals. The differences are important since each type calls for specific approaches to both teaching and assessment.
- Since young people can now access much of the world's information on a smartphone, modern education should prepare learners for transfer (i.e., to be able to *apply* their learning to new situations). We recommend that educators plan the curriculum

backward from long-term transfer goals—both within and across academic disciplines.

- Developing the brain's executive functions is both a means and an end to enduring learning. When you plan backward from long-term transfer goals while concurrently developing the skill sets needed for goal attainment, (1) learners will develop and deepen the conceptual understandings needed to transfer their learning, and (2) their brain's neural networks associated with executive function skill sets will strengthen, resulting in the lifelong skill of being self-directed learners and goal achievers.

Questions and Answers

What are the executive functions, and how do they develop?

The neural networks that direct executive functions develop in the prefrontal cortex. They begin their extended maturation starting in early childhood and continue to develop at an accelerated rate through the school years. These networks are what give students increasing voluntary control over their attention focus, inhibitory control, delay of gratification, emotional self-awareness and self-management, interpersonal relationships, goal-directed behavior, planning, prioritizing, critical thinking, judgment, reasoning, flexibility of thinking, and adaptability. Through the neuroplastic response, by which using a network makes it stronger, all these executive functions can be strengthened by classroom opportunities that guide them, across the curriculum, in foundational skillsets they then apply to their construction of understanding and transfer of knowledge.

What is the difference between Knowledge and Understanding?

Knowledge refers to the "knowing" of facts, vocabulary, and basic concepts, and it can be thought of as "binary" (i.e., you either know it or you don't). *Understanding* involves comprehension of abstract and transferrable ideas (concepts, principles, and processes) and can be thought of in terms of degrees (i.e., one can have a deep understanding, a surface [incomplete] understanding, and a misunderstanding). A student can know a fact (e.g., the date of the *Brown v. Board of Education of Topeka* Supreme Court ruling) without understanding its meaning.

Another distinction between the terms is realized when we consider assessment. To see if a student "knows" information, teachers can use objective questions with correct answers. However, understanding is best assessed by having students *apply* their learning to a new situation (transfer) and *explain* their reasoning.

4

Brain-Friendly Assessment Practices

For educators, the word *assessment* may conjure up thoughts of the annual period of high-stakes, accountability testing; or the term may cause them to focus on the classroom measures they will use to evaluate the learning of their students. For learners, the word *assessment* may lead them to think about how they will be graded or what will happen if their grades drop. For high school students, the word may evoke the stressful periods of college admissions tests or final exams. Although such reactions are not surprising, they reflect a limited view of assessment and its potential for enhancing learning, not just measuring and grading it. In this chapter, we'll consider different purposes and forms of assessment and present practical ways of using each to contribute to what the brain needs for optimal leaning.

The Purposes for Assessment

Form follows function. Before speaking about specific assessment practices that align with the neuroscience of learning, let's step back and take a broader view of assessment. In general, we can distinguish two broad purposes for educational assessments: evaluation and feedback.

Assessments used for evaluation (sometimes known as *summative* assessments) measure the extent to which learners have achieved targeted goals and typically serve as the basis for grading. Evaluative assessments are also used to make programmatic decisions, including promotion/retention or admission into programs (such as advanced placement courses), higher education, or the workplace.

A second broad purpose for assessment is to provide feedback to teachers and students to inform actions taken to improve learning.

Often referred to as *formative,* these assessments include pre-assessments, used at the beginning of a new unit or lesson to determine prior knowledge and skill levels, and ongoing assessments that are used throughout instruction to gauge whether students are "getting it" and to guide instructional interventions. Assessment expert Rick Stiggins (2004) characterizes these two different types of assessments as assessments *of* learning and assessments *for* learning, respectively. Figure 4.1 summarizes these various purposes for classroom assessments.

Figure 4.1 Purposes for Classroom Assessment

Evaluative Assessments *of* Learning	Formative Assessments *for* Learning	
Summative Assessments	**Pre-assessments**	**Ongoing Assessments**
Summative assessments are more formal and evaluative in nature, generally resulting in a score or a grade. These assessments are typically conducted toward the end of a unit, course, or grade level to determine the degree of mastery or proficiency according to identified learning targets. Their results may be made public (e.g., on report cards).	Pre-assessments *precede* instruction on a new topic in order to check students' prior knowledge and experience, skill levels, and potential misconceptions. Pre-assessments can also be used to get to know students' interests, talents and/or learning preferences. Pre-assessments provide information to assist teacher planning and guide differentiated instruction.	Ongoing assessments provide feedback to learners and teachers in order to improve learning and performance. Formative assessments include both formal (e.g., a quiz) and informal methods (e.g., a teacher's observation as students work). Because their purpose is to *inform,* the results of formative assessments should generally not be used for grading nor made public.
Examples: unit test, performance task, final exam, culminating project or performance, "best works" portfolio	*Examples:* pre-test, survey, KWL, skill checks, observations, interest surveys	*Examples:* oral questioning, teachers' observations, review of draft work, think-alouds by students, exit cards

The Understanding by Design framework acknowledges these various purposes for assessment by treating them differently in Stages 2 and 3 of backward design. In Stage 2, teachers identify the assessments that will show the extent to which students have achieved the goals identified in Stage 1. These assessments of learning are evaluative (summative) in nature and are the basis for grading. In Stage 3 of backward design, teachers develop the learning plan for the unit; this is where formative assessments for learning—both pre- and ongoing—are included. We will now explore how educators can use these different assessments—pre-assessments, ongoing assessments, and evaluative assessments—to enhance student learning and performance.

Pre-assessments

Effective teachers don't begin teaching a new unit until they have determined the prior knowledge and skill levels of their learners. The rationale for the importance of pre-assessment has been solidly grounded in research from cognitive psychology:

> In the most general sense, the contemporary view of learning is that people construct new knowledge and understandings based on what they already know and believe... A logical extension of the view that new knowledge must be constructed from existing knowledge is that teachers need to pay attention to the incomplete understandings, the false beliefs, and the naïve renditions of concepts that learners bring with them to a given subject. (Bransford et al., 2000, p. 114)

Because new learning builds upon a base of previously stored knowledge, teachers must determine what students know (or think they know) about a new concept or process before layering on new information. Using pre-assessments, a teacher can discover which students may have skills gaps or hold misconceptions. This information guides decisions about where to begin and what differentiation may be needed to accommodate the varied knowledge and skill levels in a class.

How Pre-assessments Activate Prior Knowledge

Pre-assessments do not simply provide information for the teacher; they can also *activate* any prior knowledge that learners may have about the topics and skills that will be addressed in upcoming lessons. Recall that the brain constructs and expands learning into memory circuits through pattern recognition. After new sensory information passes through the amygdala en route to the upper brain, it enters the hippocampus, where it is retained for less than a minute. Once this new information enters the hippocampus, it must connect with related memories if it is to be encoded into short-term memory and ultimately retained as long-term memory. Successful construction of short-term memory results from this consolidation in the hippocampus of new sensory input with related prior knowledge activated from storage. This system of storing and matching information by patterns is why pre-assessments can activate related prior-knowledge memory circuits and facilitate the linking of new information in short-term memory.

Pre-assessment Techniques

Practically speaking, there are a number of specific and efficient techniques that teachers can use to pre-assess prior knowledge and skills while concurrently "preheating" (activating) associated memory networks. Four of the most widely used pre-assessments that can be applied across subjects and grades are KWL organizers, pre-tests, skill checks, and interest surveys.

KWL. Typically taking the form of a three-column organizer, the KWL technique works like this: Before introducing a new topic or skill, teachers ask students what they already **K**now (or think they know) about it. Students' ideas are recorded on a board or chart paper under the K column. Secondly, teachers ask them what they **W**ant to know (or what questions they have) about the new topic or skill. These are recorded under the W column. (Students' questions may reveal interests that can be used to "hook" them to the topic.) As the lesson or unit proceeds, **L**earnings are summarized and recorded in the L column. Because the L column summarizes key learnings, it can be used as a study guide for the unit.

Note: Sometimes students make initial statements (K) that are incorrect, or their statements or questions (W) reveal misconceptions. Clearly, it is better to reveal these at the beginning of a new unit so that the teacher can address the errors or misunderstandings *during* the unit rather than discover them on the final unit assessment!

Pre-test. Teachers can use a pre-test to check prior knowledge of key facts and concepts. We recommend easy-to-give, easy-to-check formats, such as multiple-choice or true-false, that quickly reveal what students already know about a topic. The results of a pre-test help teachers plan instruction, select instructional resources, and determine the need for differentiation.

A worthwhile addition to a pre-test is the inclusion of items that check for possible misconceptions. For example, present students with common errors or predictable misconceptions on a designated topic, concept, or process to see if they can detect the error or misconception.

Skill checks. Athletic coaches generally open a season with try-outs, during which they assess the skill and conditioning levels of potential players. They use this valuable information to plan subsequent practices that will have maximum effect on players' performance. Although classroom teachers, unlike coaches, do not have the luxury of "cutting" students, they can nonetheless employ skill checks that allow students to demonstrate their current proficiency level with a targeted skill or process. We recommend using a proficiency checklist or developmental rubric when assessing the degree of skill competence. Students can then use the same checklist or rubric to gauge their progress during the unit via self- and peer assessments. Because these pre-assessments have a different purpose than evaluative assessments, it is important to let students know that the results will *not* be counted toward final grades.

Interest surveys. Another type of pre-assessment is particularly well suited to use at the beginning of a school year (as well as when new students enroll during the year) as a means of getting to know students—their interests, talents, prior experiences, personalities, and preferred ways of learning. See Chapter 7 for more details about, and examples of, such "getting-to-know-you" pre-assessments.

Ongoing Assessments

In addition to using pre-assessments at the start of a new unit, teachers who regularly use formative assessments can provide the feedback that students need to deepen their learning and improve their performance. The significance of ongoing assessments for learning was documented 20 years ago by British researchers Paul Black and Dylan Wiliam (1998), who conducted a meta-analysis of over 250 studies from several countries. They concluded that when used properly, formative assessment is one of the most significant teacher actions for guiding classroom decisions and improving student learning. These benefits are confirmed by a meta-analysis of more than 800 studies of factors influencing student achievement conducted by John Hattie (2008). Hattie noted that 3 of the top 10 interventions having the greatest effect on learning were the use of formative assessments, providing timely feedback to learners, and engaging students in self-assessment.

These findings are consistent with the experience of video gamers, as we have discussed. One of the central features that make video games so compelling to players is the immediate feedback that the game provides. Classroom teachers can emulate this feature of video games by using ongoing, formative assessments to provide feedback to guide their teaching and support student learning. A variety of ongoing assessment techniques may be used to monitor the learning pulses of students, including the following.

Observations. Perhaps the most natural formative assessment occurs through "kid watching." Teachers who carefully observe students as they work invariably notice areas of strengths (when students are "getting it") as well as points of weakness. This information helps them determine if they need to reteach the entire class or work with a subgroup of learners who are struggling. In some cases—in physical education, for example—teachers rely on a list of predeveloped performance indicators to guide their observations of a newly learned skill.

All-pupil responses. Formative assessment can be as simple as asking a question and analyzing a student's response. Although teachers can, of course, ask questions of individuals to check for understanding, we also recommend posing questions and prompts that will elicit responses from an entire class. Students can respond via hand signals (thumbs up or down), write their answers on mini-whiteboards, or use a smartphone app or clicker device. (In the latter case, teachers can tabulate the results on their computer to provide immediate feedback.) Here are examples of quick checks for understanding that teachers can use with a group of learners:

- Prediction—*What number should appear next in the sequence?*
- Agree/disagree—*Is this an example of alliteration?*
- True-or-false misconception check—*It is colder in winter in the Northern Hemisphere because the sun is farther away from the earth.*

Dend-writes and exit cards. Dend-writes is a "brainy" term (pun intended) for brief writing prompts used to elicit summaries or questions from students about newly introduced material. Teachers can use them at the beginning or the middle of a class, whereas exit cards are typically completed at the end of a class period or week. Here are sample prompts:

- *What are the most important things you learned about ________?*
- *What do you understand about ________?*
- *What don't you understand yet? What questions do you have?*

Teachers then scan the responses, looking for patterns—such as when students have the same questions or reveal some common misconceptions—that provide feedback about the impact of their teaching and inform needed instructional adjustments.

Concept map. A concept map offers a graphic representation that depicts the relationship among concepts. Teachers can ask students to create a web or concept map to show the elements or components of a topic or process. This formative assessment technique is especially effective at revealing the extent to which students understand the connections among the elements or have gaps in their knowledge.

Colored cups. In this simple way to obtain self-assessment information from students, teachers distribute small plastic cups of different colors and ask students to place the cups on their desk according to their degree of understanding during a lesson (green = *I've got it*; yellow = *I'm not sure*; red = *I'm lost*). Using this technique, teachers can quickly respond to the students who need help—for example, by inviting the greens to assist the yellows while the teacher works with the reds.

Return of draft work with feedback. A well-established formative assessment process used by teachers of English and visual arts is to have students submit a draft of their writing or sketches of proposed drawings or paintings that the teacher reviews and returns with written or oral feedback. Students then have the opportunity to revise or refine their work and submit a final version.

Question box/board. Another simple formative assessment technique involves establishing a location—such as a question box, a bulletin board, or a class website—where students may post questions about things that they do not understand. Students who are uncomfortable admitting publicly that they do not understand will appreciate this technique.

All these formative assessment techniques are efficient yet revealing. They provide feedback to both teachers and learners that can enhance learning. Just remember once again: it is critical that students understand that their responses to formative assessments will not be graded. The assessments are intended to inform, not evaluate!

Feedback That the Brain Can Use

Although the benefits of formative assessments are well established, Wiggins (2012) identifies several qualities that must be present for the associated feedback to be most useful to learners. They include the following:

1. *Feedback must be timely.* Students benefit most from feedback that they can apply right away. Although teachers cannot always provide immediate feedback like that offered electronically by a video game, the principle is clear: sooner is better than later. Waiting a week or more to find out how you did on a quiz is not likely to help your learning.
2. *Feedback must be specific and descriptive.* Some teachers think that by giving a grade (C+), a score (78%), or a general comment ("Good job!" or "Try harder"), they are providing feedback. Unfortunately, these all fail the specificity test. Effective feedback must be more specific, highlighting explicit strengths as well as areas of weaknesses; for example, "Your persuasive essay was well organized and addressed your audience. However, you did not support your claim with relevant evidence."
3. *Feedback must be understandable and actionable.* Feedback is useful only if it can be acted on by the learner, so teachers must be careful to use student-friendly language that their students can follow. For example, instead of saying, "Document your reasoning process," a teacher could say, "Show your work in a step-by-step manner so others can follow your thinking." McTighe and O'Connor (2005) propose a straightforward test for classroom feedback: "Can the learners tell *specifically* from the given feedback what they have done well and what they could do next time to improve? If not, then the feedback is not specific or understandable enough for the learner" (p. 14).
4. *Feedback must allow for self-adjustment.* Providing learners with timely and specific feedback is necessary but insufficient. Researchers Bransford, Brown, and Cocking (2000) highlight this crucial feature: "Feedback is most valuable when students have the opportunity to use it to revise their thinking as they are working on a unit or project" (p. 141). To ensure that students benefit

from feedback, they must have opportunities to refine, revise, and practice based on the formative feedback.

The virtues of feedback are documented by Richard Light (2001), a professor at Harvard University, who interviewed college graduates about the most effective courses that they had taken during their undergraduate experience. Here is a summary of his findings as reported in his book, *Making the Most Out of College: Students Speak Their Minds*:

> The big point—it comes up over and over again as crucial—is the importance of quick and detailed feedback. Students overwhelmingly report that the single most important ingredient for making a course effective is getting rapid response on assignments and quizzes.... An overwhelming majority are convinced that their best learning takes place when they have a chance to submit an early version of their work, get detailed feedback and criticism, and then hand in a final revised version. (p. 103).

Learning from feedback is an important aspect of constructing memories and building executive function. The school years show progressive improvements in the brain's neural feedback-learning network. Brain imaging and neuroelectric studies reveal increased activity in memory construction and memory retrieval regions and in the executive function networks in the prefrontal cortex during feedback-based learning. This activity is not seen during observational learning when no feedback or guidance is provided (Hiebert et al., 2014; Peters et al., 2014).

Self- and Peer Assessment

A key component of formative assessment is the involvement of students in the assessment process (Brookhart & McTighe, 2017). In a world of rapid change, exponential expansion of knowledge, and nearly instantaneous access to the world's information, it is impossible for schools to impart all of the knowledge that today's learners will need in the future. Accordingly, developing students' capacities for self-directed learning should become a high-priority goal of a modern education. Central to self-direction are the brain's executive functions, including the ability to focus one's attention, monitor one's actions, and use feedback to make adjustments when necessary.

Teachers can cultivate these functions in students by providing opportunities for them to regularly self-assess their work and set new achievement goals. A natural way to do this is through the use of metacognitive prompts such as the following, suggested by Wiggins and McTighe (2012):

- *What was most effective in ________?*
- *What was least effective in ________?*
- *How could you improve ________?*
- *What would you do differently next time?*
- *What are you most proud of?*
- *What are you most disappointed in?*
- *How difficult was ________ for you?*
- *What are your strengths in ________ ?*
- *What are your deficiencies in ________ ?*
- *What questions do you still have about ________?*
- *How does your preferred way(s) of learning influence ________?*
- *What grade/score do you deserve? Why?*
- *How does what you've learned connect to other learnings?*
- *How has what you've learned changed your thinking?*
- *How does what you've learned relate to the present and future?*
- *What do you want to learn next?* (p. 52)

Another way to reinforce self-assessment and goal setting is to include students in parent-teacher conferences. In student-involved conferencing, learners take an active role in reviewing their work in front of their parents, and with the teacher's guidance, they set specific achievement goals for the future. This practice can yield two benefits: (1) parents will be better able to support their child's academic growth if they are aware of agreed-upon goals, and (2) the child is exercising important executive functions.

The inclination and ability to self-assess and reflect does not emerge automatically in most children and adolescents. Parents and teachers need to encourage these executive functions both at home and at school. In the classroom, teachers can overtly model the processes of self-assessment and goal setting by thinking aloud and reinforcing students as they attempt to self-assess and set goals on their own. Over time, as with any learned skill, we expect students to become increasingly capable of honest self-assessment and effective adjustment.

Evaluative Assessments

A third type of assessment is evaluative, or summative, in nature. These assessments are used to gauge the extent to which students have reached targeted learning goals and serve as a basis for grading. When planning evaluative assessments in Stage 2 of backward design, teachers are called upon to "think like assessors" and ask themselves this question: *Given the learning goals identified in Stage 1, what evidence will show that my students have achieved these desired results?*

We have observed that teachers are often most comfortable in assessing knowledge and skills using familiar objective-test formats, such as multiple-choice, matching, true-false, or fill-in-the-blank. These formats can certainly provide appropriate assessment evidence when we want to see if students know factual information, such as multiplication tables or the capitals of European countries. Similarly, when assessing proficiency in a skill, such as riding a bike or drawing from observation, a simple skill demonstration or product review will offer valid evidence.

However, the goals of understanding and transfer require different measures than test items with a single correct answer or demonstrations of simple skills. Consider these questions: *What evidence will show that students genuinely understand abstract concepts and complex processes? How will we determine if they can transfer their learning to a new situation?* As a general rule, we propose that the goals of understanding and transfer are most appropriately assessed through performance assessment tasks that ask students to *apply* their learning to a new situation and provide an explanation or justification. Teachers can use supplementary evidence (usually obtained through more traditional tests and quizzes) to assess the acquisition of discrete knowledge and skills. In Understanding by Design, these distinctions are reflected in the UbD Template (see Figure 2.1) for Stage 2, where you'll see two broad categories of evaluative assessments: Performance Tasks and Supplementary Evidence.

A key principle of the UbD backward design process is alignment; that is, that the evaluative assessments identified in Stage 2 closely align to the various learning goals targeted in Stage 1. A lack of alignment signals that the assessments may not provide valid measures. McTighe (2013) recommends a simple way of checking the alignment between the Stage 2 assessments and the identified learning goals. Simply specify the assessments that you plan to use to determine if the targeted learning has been achieved. Then show your proposed unit assessments in Stage 2 (but *not* the Stage 1 goals) to another teacher or team, and ask them to tell you what they believe the learning goals must be, based only on their look at your assessments. This "alignment check" can be done quickly and informally, but it offers wonderfully specific and actionable feedback to help improve your assessment alignment, if need be.

Using Performance-Based Assessments to Both Motivate and Measure

Performance-based assessments yield tangible products and performances. This assessment format is widely used in physical education, the visual and performing arts, and career technology, where performance is the natural focus of learning and instruction. When understanding and transfer are among the goals (as UbD expects), we recommend the regular use of such performance assessments in *all* subjects. Because performance assessments call for students to apply their learning to new situations—that is, to transfer—such assessments can provide evidence of understanding within and across the disciplines. Moreover, performance-based assessments can also elicit the 21st century skills of critical thinking, creativity, and cooperation, along with habits of mind, such as precision and perseverance. Typically, performance assessments are presented to learners as tasks. Here are two examples:

> Evaluate a Claim
>
> The Pooper Scooper Kitty Litter Company claims that their litter is 40 percent more absorbent than other brands. You are a consumer-advocates researcher who has been asked to evaluate their claim. Develop a plan for conducting the investigation. Your plan should be specific enough so that the lab investigators could follow it to evaluate the claim.

> Make Your Case
>
> You have an idea that you believe will make your school better, and you want to convince school leaders that they should act on your idea. Identify your audience (e.g., principal, PTSA board, students) and do the following:

1. Describe your idea.
2. Explain why and how it will improve the school.
3. Develop a plan for acting on your idea.

Your idea and plan can be communicated to your target audience in a letter, an e-mail, or a presentation.

Authentic Tasks

As already noted, one of the long-term aims of Understanding by Design is equipping students with the ability to transfer their learning—to be able to apply what they have learned flexibly and effectively to address new and genuine issues and problems that they will encounter within and outside school. With this goal in mind, we recommend that teachers strive to establish authentic contexts for their assessments and assignments. Such tasks tend to be more meaningful and motivating for students, while also providing teachers with assessment evidence of understanding and transfer. Grant Wiggins (2006) offers a succinct description of authenticity:

> What do I mean by "authentic assessment"? It's simply performances and product requirements that are faithful to real-world demands, opportunities, and constraints. The students are tested on their ability to "do" the subject in context, to transfer their learning effectively.

The idea of authenticity can be exemplified through a sports analogy. Think of the difference between practices and a game. Practices often focus on developing the skills of the sport through individual skill drills, whereas the game is inherently unpredictable—that is, players are faced with ever-changing situations and they must transfer the skills they have practiced against an opponent. Too often in classrooms, we see an overemphasis on tests that are the equivalent of decontextualized drills, with few, if any, opportunities for students to actually "play the game" or "do" the subject in an authentic manner.

The GRASPS Elements

Performance tasks can establish relevant contexts that reflect genuine goals and authentic applications of knowledge. Wiggins and McTighe

(2012) have developed a practical tool for teachers to use in designing more authentic tasks by considering the elements in the acronym GRASPS. Here are the elements for each letter: (1) a real-world **G**oal, (2) a meaningful **R**ole for the student, (3) an authentic (or simulated) **A**udience, (4) a contextualized **S**ituation that involves real-world application, (5) student-generated culminating **P**roducts and **P**erformances, and (6) the **S**uccess criteria by which student products and performances will be judged. Figure 4.2 provides a GRASPS worksheet to illustrate the idea.

Here is an example of a performance task used as part of the study of a state or province. Can you recognize the GRASPS elements contained within the task prompt?

> A group of nine foreign students is visiting your school for one month as part of an international exchange program. (Don't worry, they speak English!) The principal has asked your class to plan and budget a four-day tour of [your state or province] to help the visitors understand the state's impact on the history and development of our nation. Plan your tour so that the visitors are shown sites that best capture the ways that [your state or province] has influenced our nation's development. You should prepare a written tour itinerary, including an explanation of why each site was selected. Include a map tracing the route for the four-day tour and a budget for the trip.

In addition to performance tasks that reflect real-world applications, teachers can heighten learners' goal buy-in by creating tasks that reflect their students' interests and experiences. For example, a high school mathematics teacher developed a task in which students compared various smartphone plans in terms of data usage and then recommended the most cost-effective plans for individuals with different needs—for example, a grandparent and a video gamer—and explained their mathematical reasoning. He found that most students were more engaged by this task than by the dry, decontextualized problems in their textbook.

In sum, performance tasks that are authentic in terms of both real-world applications and personal interests can increase students' motivation, their willingness to apply effort, and their receptiveness to the associated lessons that will prepare them for the task.

Figure 4.2 GRASPS Worksheet

Goal:

- Your task in the situation is ____________________
- Your goal is to ____________________
- The problem or challenge is ____________________
- The obstacle to overcome is ____________________

Role:

- You are ____________________
- You have been asked to ____________________
- Your job is ____________________

Audience:

- The target audience is ____________________
- Your clients are ____________________
- You need to convince ____________________

Situation:

- The situation you find yourself in is ____________________
- The challenge involves dealing with ____________________

Product or Performance and Purpose:

- You will create a __________ in order to ____________________
- You need to develop __________ so that ____________________

Success Criteria:

- Your performance needs to ____________________
- Your work will be judged by ____________________
- Your product must meet the following criteria ____________________
- A successful result will ____________________

____

Source: From *Understanding by Design Guide to Advanced Concepts in Creating and Reviewing Units* (p. 80), by G. Wiggins and J. McTighe, 2012, Alexandria, VA: ASCD. Copyright 2012 by G. Wiggins and J. McTighe. Adapted with permission.

Differentiating Performance Tasks

As previously discussed in the video game model, learners who believe that they can be at least somewhat successful on a given task—that it is an achievable challenge—are more likely to try. However, a class of students is likely to vary considerably in terms of prior knowledge, skill levels, interests, and preferred ways of demonstrating learning. Some students are adept at writing; others prefer to explain concepts orally or visually. Allowing students to work to their strengths on an assessment can increase their potential to succeed, yet (if the options are carefully determined) still provide evidence of their learning. A standardized, one-size-fits-all approach to classroom assessment may be efficient, but not all students will necessarily see it as worthwhile or achievable for them. One way to address this variability is to differentiate tasks when appropriate.

Tomlinson and McTighe (2006) suggest using the GRASPS format for task differentiation. By varying the GRASPS elements, teachers can adjust the difficulty levels and allow student choice, while still obtaining the assessment evidence they need. Here is an example: Consider a standard for a health class that calls for a basic understanding of "balanced diet." Evidence of this understanding could be obtained by having students explain the concept, present examples of balanced and unbalanced meals, and list health problems that might result from a nutritionally imbalanced diet. A teacher could collect such evidence in writing, but this requirement would be inappropriate for a learner with dysgraphia or an ESL student with limited skills in written English. Indeed, some students' difficulty with writing could cause the teacher to incorrectly infer that they do not understand the concept of a balanced diet.

Now look at three versions of this task using variations in several of the GRASPS elements:

Version 1

- *Goal*—Explain the concept of a balanced diet and give examples of at least two health problems that could result from poor nutrition
- *Role*—Yourself
- *Audience*—Kids your age
- *Situation*—Teaching others about healthful eating
- *Product/performance*—An illustrated brochure
- *Success criteria*—Accurate and complete information presented, clear and understandable to the audience

Version 2

- *Goal*—Explain the concept of a balanced diet and give examples of at least two health problems that could result from poor nutrition
- *Role*—Yourself
- *Audience*—Kindergarten children
- *Situation*—Teaching others about healthful eating
- *Product/performance*—A picture book and oral explanation
- *Success criteria*—Accurate and complete information presented, clear and understandable to the audience

Version 3

- *Goal*—Explain the concept of a balanced diet and give examples of at least two health problems that could result from poor nutrition
- *Role*—A nutrition expert
- *Audience*—Adults and teenagers
- *Situation*—Teaching others about healthful eating
- *Product/performance*—A written brochure for supermarket check-out stands and health clinics
- *Success criteria*—Accurate and complete information presented, clear and understandable to the audience

Notice in these examples that a performance task can differ in terms of role, audience, and products/performances while still obtaining appropriate assessment evidence. Notice also that the goal and the success criteria are *not* modified. In other words, the assessment needs to see evidence that students understand the concept of a balanced diet and recognize health problems that could result from poor nutrition. Similarly, regardless of how they show this understanding—orally, pictorially, or in writing—they must meet the *same* success criteria. In this way, teachers can gather needed assessment evidence while still allowing flexibility for students.

Although we encourage teachers to look for opportunities to differentiate performance tasks whenever possible, we offer the following cautions:

- Don't forget that the goal of an assessment is to collect evidence of learning based on the targeted outcomes, not to offer a "cool" menu of assessment choices. Your goals will determine what evidence is needed and help you decide if or when differentiation is appropriate. For example, for a unit on public speaking, students will need to speak before an audience even if they might be uncomfortable doing so. Nonetheless, a speech teacher could offer the students some choices—for example, on topic or audience—and still obtain the needed evidence.

- Differentiation of performance tasks or learning activities is a worthy goal, but it must be feasible. It is unrealistic (and probably unmanageable) to have 30 students producing 30 different products, and so teachers must balance the ideal of personalization with the reality of practicality (and their sanity).
- When using authentic performance assessments, it is important that "the juice is worth the squeeze." Performance tasks typically take time for students to prepare and produce; they also take more teacher time to score. In some cases, we have seen tasks that do not pass the squeeze test (for example, students dressing up as historical figures to present historical information). If the assessment goal is to see if students know facts of history, we recommend using an easy-to-give, quick-to-score multiple-choice test rather than a "dress up" performance task. Reserve performance assessments for goals that require understanding and transfer, not recall.

Using Rubrics to Enhance Student Performance

Authentic performance assessments are typically open-ended and do not have a single correct answer or solution process. Thus, rather than relying on an answer key or a Scantron machine, teachers should evaluate students' performances using established criteria linked to the targeted learning outcomes being assessed. Criteria serve as the base for the development of a more detailed *rubric*, a scoring tool for evaluating student work according to a performance scale. For example, a rubric might specify 1, 2, or 3 points for work that shows various levels of quality.

Two types of rubrics—holistic and analytic—are widely used to judge student products and performances on open-ended performance tasks and projects. A *holistic* rubric provides an overall impression of a student's work, typically yielding a single score, rating, or grade for a product or performance. Figure 4.3 presents an example of a holistic rubric for a graphic display of data.

Figure 4.3 Holistic Rubric for a Graphic Display of Data	
3	All data are accurately represented on the graph. All parts of the graph (e.g., units of measurement, rows) are correctly labeled. The graph contains a title that clearly tells what the data show. The graph is very neat and easy to read.
2	All data are accurately represented on the graph, OR the graph contains minor errors. All parts of the graph are correctly labeled, OR the graph contains minor inaccuracies. The graph contains a title that suggests what the data show. The graph is generally neat and readable.
1	The data are inaccurately represented, contain major errors, OR are missing. Only some parts of the graph are correctly labeled, OR labels are missing. The title does not reflect what the data show, OR the title is missing. The graph is sloppy and difficult to read.

An *analytic* rubric, like that shown in Figure 4.4, divides a product or performance into distinct traits or dimensions, with each evaluated separately, although an overall score can be derived. Notice the difference between the holistic rubric shown in Figure 4.3 and the analytic version presented in Figure 4.4.

Figure 4.4 Analytic Rubric for a Graphic Display of Data

	Title	Labels	Accuracy	Neatness
3	The graph contains a title that clearly tells what the data show.	All parts of the graph (e.g., units of measurement, rows) are correctly labeled.	All data are accurately represented on the graph.	The graph is very neat and easy to read.
2	The graph contains a title that suggests what the data show.	Some parts of the graph are inaccurately labeled.	Data representation contains minor errors.	The graph is generally neat and readable.
1	The title does not reflect what the data show, OR the title is missing.	Only some parts of the graph are correctly labeled, OR labels are missing.	The data are inaccurately represented, contain major errors, OR are missing.	The graph is sloppy and difficult to read.

Given these two types of rubrics, which one should teachers use? Here's our general recommendation: If your main goal is to obtain an overall rating or final grade, then holistic rubrics will do. However, when you want to provide detailed feedback on the important traits of a performance, analytic rubrics are needed. Given our discussion of the video game model and the brain's need for timely and specific feedback, you should not be surprised that we strongly recommend the use of analytic rubrics for classroom assessments. Here are the reasons:

- Analytic rubrics can provide specific feedback on qualitatively different but salient traits of performance. In contrast, a holistic rubric provides only a score (*3*) or a grade (*C*), and neither of these embody the qualities of effective feedback previously discussed.
- Rubrics can serve as more than just evaluative tools to measure and grade student learning at the end of instruction. Teachers can use rubrics as learning targets at the start to help learners recognize the qualities needed to achieve instructional goals.
- From a neurological perspective, rubrics provide a template onto which students can link new learning when their brains recognize the categories of stored knowledge it relates to (Goodrich, 1996–1997).
- The use of analytic rubrics can foster the development of a growth mindset by helping students see the relationship between their effort and their progress or achievement.
- Students can use analytic rubrics for self- and peer assessment, thereby developing the executive functions of goal directing, critical analyzing, and self-monitoring.

Tips for Designing and Using Rubrics

Many rubrics are available in textbooks and online; however, not all of these rubrics are sound. Here are suggestions for ensuring that the rubrics you use will provide clarity for students and reliable evaluation for teachers.

1. Before writing the rubric, consider the learning goals for which the performance task is targeted, as well as what the ideal end product would look like if these goals were achieved. Then, make sure that the rubric includes the most salient traits, given the purpose of the

assessment and the qualities of excellent performance. Ask yourself these questions:

- *Does the rubric only contain traits that are easiest to score (e.g., word count, correct computation) rather than all important traits (e.g., organization of ideas, mathematical reasoning)?*
- *Could a student get high scores without really demonstrating the desired understandings or producing excellent work?*

2. Use kid-friendly language, especially for younger students, so that they will understand.

3. Present the rubric early in a new unit or in conjunction with a performance task so that students have clear goals for their work. Well-defined criteria provide a clear description of quality performance so that students will not have to guess what is most important or how teachers will judge their work. The greater the clarity of the expectations in the rubric, the more likely the students will feel capable of succeeding.

4. Providing a rubric to students in advance of the assessment is a necessary, but often insufficient, condition to support their performance. Along with the rubric, we strongly recommend showing models or examples of student work to illustrate the different levels of a rubric. Sometimes known as *anchors*, these provide concrete illustrations of the key criteria and the differences across the performance scale. Learners are more likely to understand the rubric when teachers show a full range of examples to display the range of performance levels from excellent to weak.

5. When offering the rubric to students at the beginning of a new assignment or unit of study, emphasize your partnership with the students as they work to achieve success. Help students see the rubric as a guide for success. Students are more engaged and confident when they see rubrics as offering a predictable process in which the outcome is clearly the result of specifically defined input. Students understand that their grades are indeed within their control; if they are willing to put in the effort, they see the path they need to follow to reach their goals.

6. Rubrics can serve as more than just an evaluation tool for teacher use. Students can use them for self- and peer assessment and goal setting. Figure 4.5 presents two simple modifications to the format of a traditional rubric (McTighe, 2013). Notice the inclusion of two tiny check boxes at the bottom of each cell of an analytic rubric. Students can use

the check boxes on the left to self-assess their work before they turn it in to the teacher. The teacher can then use the other box to record the "official" evaluation.

Figure 4.5 Analytic Rubric for Public Speaking

	Volume	Rate of Speech/ Pacing	Eye Contact	Posture
4	Speaker projects with a strong, clear voice that can easily be heard by all. ☐ ☐	Speech is delivered at a comfortable and appropriate pace. ☐ ☐	Speaker establishes and maintains excellent eye contact throughout. ☐ ☐	Speaker maintains excellent posture, displaying both confidence and composure. ☐ ☐
3	Speaker speaks at a volume that can generally be heard without strain. ☐ ☐	Speech is delivered at an appropriate pace, with occasional pauses. ☐ ☐	Speaker makes eye contact with the audience but has occasional lapses. ☐ ☐	Speaker maintains good posture and composure. ☐ ☐
2	Speaker uses a soft voice that makes it difficult to hear the message. ☐ ☐	Speech is too slow or too fast, with frequent pauses. ☐ ☐	Speaker makes intermittent eye contact with the audience. ☐ ☐	Speaker displays poor posture and displays a lack of confidence. ☐ ☐
1	Speaker speaks extremely softly and/or mumbles so that the message cannot be heard or understood. ☐ ☐	Speech is halting and uneven, with long pauses, OR speech is delivered so rapidly that the audience cannot follow it. ☐ ☐	Speaker makes little or no eye contact with the audience. ☐ ☐	Speaker slouches and fidgets, displaying extreme discomfort and lack of confidence. ☐ ☐

Goals and Actions for Improvement:

Source: From *Core Learning: Assessing What Matters Most*, by J. McTighe, 2013, Salt Lake City, UT: School Improvement Network. ©2013, J. McTighe. Used with permission.

Once the performance task is scored and returned, students can compare their self-assessment with their teacher's ratings. If the two judgments do not match, teachers can use this as an opportunity to discuss the criteria, expectations, and performance standards with the learner. The goal, over time, is for students to become more discerning and able to accurately self-assess the criteria and performance scale in a rubric.

Note the insertion of a "Goals and Actions" box at the bottom of the rubric. Once their work is returned with feedback, students are then expected to identify one or more goals for the future or actions that they will take to improve their performance. This simple addition can upgrade a rubric from being solely an evaluation instrument for scoring or grading to being a practical tool for feedback, self-assessment, and goal setting.

Guiding Students in Rubric Development

Rubric design need not be the sole province of adults. Teachers can guide students in developing a rubric for a given performance task or assignment. In so doing, students often become more engaged in the assessment process and more attuned to the evaluative criteria that they identify. Initially, teachers may need to direct this process, as young people often lack the expertise to be able to determine the most important traits of a product or performance. Not surprisingly, they will often identify surface characteristics, such as neatness, spelling, or word length, and must be helped to recognize the more sophisticated dimensions, such as isolation of variables in a science experiment, or attention to audience in an oral presentation. One practical way to help them understand the key performance qualities is to show them a range of samples of previously produced products or performances and ask them to sort the samples into three or four groups based on quality. Then, have them closely examine each group and guide them in picking out the distinguishing qualities that differentiate the levels. With practice, students will improve their ability to generate a quality rubric; in doing so they will have greater understanding and ownership over the evaluation process.

Longitudinal Rubrics

A third type of rubric—longitudinal—describes growth along a novice-expert continuum, with each level representing a key benchmark on the road to expert-level performance. A nonacademic example of a longitudinal rubric may be seen in the nine different colored belts distinguishing the various proficiency levels in karate. The American Council on the Teaching of Foreign Languages (ACTFL) has developed sets of longitudinal proficiency rubrics for listening, speaking, reading, and writing that can be used in conjunction with assessments in world languages (see www.sil.org/lingualinks/LANGUAGELEARNING/OtherResources/ACTFLProficiencyGuidelines/contents.htm).

Longitudinal rubrics are especially well-suited to profiling current performance levels (regardless of age or grade) and charting student progress over time and across the grades—for example, in language arts, world languages, and physical education.

Allowing for Revision and Retakes in Evaluative Assessments

Too often, evaluative assessments such as a unit test or a final exam are used as one-shot summative events whose results are recorded indelibly. We propose that teachers consider such assessments as providers of provisional (but not final) evidence of learning and allow students at least one opportunity to make revisions or try again, based on feedback from the assessment. Here is an example: After taking a math test, a teacher returns student papers with errors marked. She then asks students to describe the type of mistakes they made on the test. Was it an error in simple computation, or does the mistake reflect confusion about a concept, such as multiplying negative numbers? After assessing where their understanding was incomplete (with teacher guidance, as needed), students specify what they will do to better learn the material, such as meet with the teacher during study hall, review textbook examples, consult an online tutorial on the topic, or practice their multiplication tables. After having put forth effort, they are allowed to retake the test.

This process gives struggling students an opportunity to improve, shows them specific ways to deepen their learning, and gives them confidence in their ability to work through challenging problems on their own. The result is a reduction in test anxiety while supporting the development of a growth mindset. Students are generally motivated to do the work to improve because they recognize this as their opportunity to be able to retake a test and improve their score or grade. A similar process can be used on more open-ended performance-based assessments, in which students receive feedback from teachers or peers on the draft products or performances, and have an opportunity to make revisions before the final version is scored.

Recall that because of the brain's self-preservation programming, it is most likely to apply its resources when it recognizes that the effort will result in a desired goal. Desired goals, as in the video game model, offer the potential for the intrinsic satisfaction and pleasure of a reward induced by dopamine (Morisano et al., 2010).

Chapter Understandings

- We recommend that educators think about assessment in ways that can enhance, not just measure and grade, student learning and performance.
- The key to assessment for learning lies in the feedback that an assessment offers to both teachers and learners.
- Pre-assessments can activate students' prior knowledge while providing teachers with insights into students' knowledge and skill levels and helping determine their achievable challenge thresholds.
- Ongoing, formative assessments can act like a video game by providing real-time feedback that students and teachers can use to improve. When learners see that they are making incremental progress toward a goal, they are more inclined to continue to put forth effort and exhibit a growth mindset.
- Although summative tests are used for evaluation and grading, teachers can make these attractive to students by including authentic performance tasks that reflect real-world applications of knowledge. By allowing students some choices for demonstrating their understanding, teachers increase opportunities for student success without lowering the bar.
- By presenting rubrics and models in advance, teachers help learners understand the success criteria, giving them clear targets for their learning and performance. And by allowing revision and

retakes, teachers acknowledge that mistakes are an accepted part of learning new things. They reinforce a growth mindset by highlighting that focused effort and persistence can lead to improvement.

Questions and Answers

Our state uses standardized tests for accountability, and these tests are all multiple choice. Why should we use more authentic performance assessments with our students when we are being judged by scores on different measures?

While this question is understandable, it reflects key misunderstandings about standardized testing (McTighe, 2016). One has to do with the belief that the best way to prepare for, and improve scores on, multiple-choice tests is to "practice" the test format. This conflates conditions for optimal learning with efficient measurement techniques. Analogously, it would be like saying that I have to "practice" for my annual physical exam to improve my health!

A related misconception is the assumption that multiple-choice items primarily test factual knowledge and basic skills; thus, drill and practice with lots of multiple-choice items will yield improved performance on standardized tests. This reasoning is flawed on two counts: (1) the most widely missed test items do *not* involve simple recall—they call for application (e.g., interpretation in reading and multistep reasoning in mathematics); and (2) most students are not engaged by multiple-choice "test-prep" worksheets. As we have noted throughout this book, if learners do not see relevance in what they are asked to do in school, they are less likely to put forth effort for learning. We contend that the best preparation for *any* test is to teach the tested content in engaging ways, involve learners in active meaning making to develop understanding, and allow them to apply their learning in authentic contexts. In sum, it doesn't matter how many practice tests we give; if the learners are not engaged or fail to see the purpose, their learning will not be optimized, and performance on high-stakes tests will not be boosted.

How do pre-assessments work in the brain to help promote memory and understanding in learners?

Pre-assessments work in multiple ways to promote the brain's responsiveness to the acquisition of new learning and construction of neural networks for long-term, durable memory and transferable conceptual understanding. As we know from the UbD framework, pre-assessments provide teachers with evidence of where students are regarding the targeted learning outcomes, so that subsequent instruction can be directed or adjusted to optimize their learning.

From our understandings of the neuroscience of learning, we know that new information must be linked to previous memory circuits for it to be encoded. Pre-assessment questions, discussions, and activities serve to activate existing memory circuits (prior knowledge) that relate to the targeted new learning. Even before students are formally taught new information, pre-assessments serve to "preheat" associated neural networks to activate related prior knowledge and focus learners' attention through curiosity and prediction.

Pre-assessments are more likely to promote the brain's responsiveness to new learning when learners are in a low-stress state. When students know the results of pre-assessments will *not* influence their grades, their unstressed brains can more readily connect to their natural response to curiosity (i.e., wanting to know what is recognized as unknown).

5

Teaching Toward AMT

In this chapter and the next, we turn our attention to the kind of instruction needed to help students acquire information and basic skills, to develop and deepen their understanding of abstract concepts and processes, and to be able to transfer their learning to new situations. We will integrate key ideas from the neuroscience of learning with the pedagogy of UbD to consider ways of teaching that can maximize academic achievement while building students' cognitive executive functions. We'll reference the video game model and present practical teaching strategies symbolized by the AMT and WHERETO acronyms from UbD and intended to do the following:

- Capture and hold learners' attention
- Help students encode new learnings into long-term memory
- Expand students' neural networks (developing and deepening understanding) by exercising the brain's executive functions
- Prepare learners to transfer their learning

When teachers plan curriculum using UbD, they identify different types of learning goals in Stage 1—knowledge and skills, understandings, and transfer goals. Wiggins and McTighe (2011) use the acronym *AMT* to symbolize these three categories of educational goals:

A = Acquisition of information and basic skills
The goal of acquiring knowledge and skill is automaticity; that is, the student should eventually be able to recall information and perform a skill on cue, without thinking.

M = Meaning making
The term *meaning making* is meant to convey the idea that understanding conceptually larger ideas requires active intellectual

work by the learner. In other words, students must try to understand something that cannot be immediately grasped, by using strategies such as looking for connections and patterns, making inferences, and forming and testing a theory. Indeed, the phrase *coming to understand* suggests a mental construction process occurring over time.

T = Transfer
Transfer refers to the ability to effectively apply learning to new situations. Having acquired knowledge and skill, and having been helped to come to understand what it means, the learner must now transfer this learning to a novel or unfamiliar context.

With clarity about goals at the start, teachers develop the learning plan in Stage 3 by considering how they will help learners *acquire* targeted knowledge and skills, *make meaning* of conceptually larger ideas, and be able to *transfer* their learning on authentic performance tasks. The AMT categories are significant because each requires different approaches to instruction and assessment. For instance, knowledge and skills can be readily transmitted through direct instruction and modeling by a teacher. However, when understanding is a goal, the teacher's role shifts from that of a dispenser of information to a facilitator of meaning making. When transfer is the goal, the teacher functions more like a coach in athletics and the arts. Learners need many opportunities to try to apply their learning in new and varied situations while the teacher/coach provides feedback. Over time, teacher support and scaffolding is gradually removed, placing greater responsibility on the students to transfer their learning autonomously.

We will now look more closely at the teaching implications of AMT. It is here that insights from the neuroscience of learning are profoundly informative.

Acquisition: Building Memories That Last

Virtually every new unit contains both declarative and procedural knowledge—information that students should *know* (declarative) and one or more skills that they should learn to *do* or improve (procedural). Acquiring these basics provides the necessary foundation for more sophisticated learning. For example, unless students have memorized the foundational vocabulary and grammatical rules of a foreign language to a needed level of automaticity, they will not have a base for building fluency. Lacking the ability to automatically activate and retrieve basic multiplication facts, students cannot progress efficiently to the multi-step process of long division. Without understanding basic terminology such as *plot, theme,* or *point of view,* students will not be able to analyze literature or discuss authors' techniques. Once students know the form and function of the main parts of a cell, such as *mitochondria, nucleus, cell wall,* and *cytoplasm,* they have the memory templates on which they can build understanding of cellular metabolism and DNA replication.

Although foundational knowledge is critical, students are sometimes expected to simply memorize facts, such as a list of academic vocabulary words presented out of context. When facts do not appear relevant or hold any personal interest, they may quickly be forgotten (sometimes immediately after the test). Neurologically, there is less growth of the brain's neural networks if circuits are activated only by asking students to repeat the same information or perform a process in the same way over and over again—for example, asking them to write a vocabulary term 10 times or solve 30 algebraic equations using the same formula. An approach that relies on rote memorization produces isolated and somewhat feeble circuits unlinked to other networks. Learners develop shallow memories and can give back only what was taught in the same way it was taught; they are unable to transfer their learning to new situations.

How, then, should we teach so that basic knowledge endures? How can we equip students to be able to recall facts and apply skills with automaticity? How can we develop connected neural networks that enable learners to transfer what they have learned? An understanding of the brain offers insights into effective teaching techniques for supporting the acquisition and encoding of new knowledge and skills into long-term memory.

Activating Prior Knowledge

The most significant variable in learning something new is prior knowledge. Thus, the likelihood of information being maintained in memory increases when students' brains are prepared in advance to "catch" the new input. This preparation requires that teachers confirm that students' foundational knowledge is accurate and then use strategies to activate the memory circuits of prior knowledge. Doing so enables the new input to physically link to the earlier circuits to construct and encode the new short-term memory. Without this pre-activation of prior knowledge, the new input has nothing to link to, and new learning, failing to consolidate with an existing circuit, is not retained. By using pre- and ongoing assessment strategies (described in Chapter 4), teachers gain information to gauge what students already know so that they can activate this prior knowledge base and reinforce the connections between new learning and students' existing memory circuits.

Here is a summary of how the brain builds memories upon existing knowledge:

- For new input to "stick," it must link to a familiar pattern. If, as new information enters the hippocampus, the brain recognizes anything similar or related to existing memories, the related memory storage networks are activated.
- These related memories are stored in multiple parts of the cerebral cortex, depending on which sensory receptors initially responded to the input. For example, the memory of ducks quacking is stored in the area of the cortex related to auditory input. Subsequently, if you were listening to a lecture about mallard ducks, the new information you were hearing would enter your hippocampus, and related past memories about ducks—such as the sound of ducks quacking, the image of ducks you saw in a pond, a fact you once heard about the properties of feathers—would "meet" the new information about mallard ducks in your hippocampus.
- The consolidation of the pre-existing related memories and the new information is the process of encoding short-term memory.
- If no prior memory is stimulated and there is nothing to meet the new input in the hippocampus, the new input, having nothing to link to, may be lost.
- Short-term memories are temporary and will be converted to long-term memories only if they are mentally manipulated in the prefrontal cortex. (Activities that require mental manipulation are described later, in the section titled "Mental Manipulation for Meaning Making.")
- Once the information has been converted to long-term memory, it will be available as prior knowledge to connect with new

information, when the relationship is recognized. Thus, when someone mentions something about a duck, your network of relational memories will be triggered and available for your brain to understand the meaning of their reference.

Extending Memory Storage and Retrieval Through Multisensory Learning

As noted in Chapter 1, none of our memories are held in single brain cells (neurons). Memory is stored in separate hemispheres of the brain, based on the sensory modality in which it is experienced. The more ways that learning is experienced and applied, the more effectively it is incorporated, stored, and retrieved from memory. When students acquire the information in a variety of ways—for example, through reading, hearing, visualization, movement—the activation of the short-term memory increases its connections (through dendrites, synapses, myelin) to construct long-term memory. Practically speaking, teachers help students build stronger and more retrievable memories by using a variety of sensory modalities when presenting information—orally, visually, in writing—as well as having students apply their learning through a variety of modalities such as writing, drawing a diagram, performing a skit, or creating a rap through which they can access all of the sensory memories (van den Heuvel, Stam, Kahn, & Hulshoff Pol, 2009).

A related idea has to do with the fact that students may have preferred ways of learning. For students who best remember things they see, the visual memory of a science demonstration or a video demonstration or experiment may be the first memory activated. From there, the connecting neural networks will activate the other cortical regions storing information related to the same topic that came from the other sensory experiences, such as a lecture or a reading from a text. In fact, one way of personalizing learning is to encourage students to become aware of their preferred ways of learning and to seek to encode and access information accordingly. Here are some examples of multisensory teaching and learning:

- After hearing and reading the definition of an electron, students could visualize electrons orbiting the nucleus of an atom, then make a buzzing sound to represent the electricity as the electron whizzes by. Or the teacher might rub a balloon against the wall and have the students hold it above the hair on their arms to experience the tingling associated with the electrons' negative charge as their hairs move. Students could then create sketches of what they visualized, felt, or did when moving around the room as electrons in their atomic orbits.

- When teaching addition and subtraction or positive and negative numbers, teachers can use words, desktop number lines, and visuals. By creating a number line on the floor, they can bring in motor memory by having students start at zero and walk to the number they are given while looking down at the numbers and counting the steps as they walk. Once they arrive at the number 5, the teacher can ask them to take one, two, or three more steps and tell what number they are now on. They could look down to confirm or look down the whole time. Later, with more knowledge, they could walk backward with the same activity for subtraction, or the number line could extend to less than zero for working with negative numbers. Classmates could write down the equations representing the movements made by the student on the number line.
- In a geology class, the teacher could bring in different kinds of rocks for students to touch and identify.
- In social studies classes, the teacher could have students engage in debates or have mock trials of famous cases, with students adopting the personas of historical figures.
- In a psychology class, the teacher could simulate a robbery in the class and later ask students questions about the robbery. Their answers will typically vary and can illustrate how eyewitness memory is flawed.

Another way to present multisensory experiences to students of any age is to bring in an expert or a professional in the field. For example, the teacher could invite a nurse to discuss different aspects of anatomy or health. The professionals or experts could bring special tools from their jobs; a nurse could bring a blood pressure cuff or a stethoscope, and students could have the opportunity to take their blood pressure or listen to each other's lungs. Experts can be particularly interesting for high school students, who are often trying to figure out what type of job or career lies in their future. By bringing in someone who works in the field, teachers not only activate more of students' senses but also give them ideas about how the knowledge they are learning will transfer to the world beyond the classroom.

Memory Scaffolds

Just as a scaffold supports the construction of a new building, memory scaffolds can enhance and support the acquisition and retention of information. Three familiar and effective scaffolds to assist students as they acquire new information and skills are mnemonics, advance organizers, and process guides.

Mnemonics

A simple way to assist student memory is through the use of mnemonic devices. Mnemonics use elaborative encoding, retrieval cues, and imagery as specific tools to encode any given information in a way that allows for efficient storage and retrieval. Mnemonics help original information become associated with something more accessible or meaningful in order to boost retention of the information. Commonly encountered mnemonic devices include short poems (e.g., "Thirty days hath September…"), acronyms (e.g., ROY-G-BIV), and the loci method (e.g., linking the rooms in a familiar building to items to be remembered). Their effectiveness reflects the fact that the brain is likely to remember things that are personal, surprising, physical, rhyming or musical, and spatial more readily than abstract or impersonal information. Teachers can suggest helpful mnemonics to help learners remember academic content, such as vocabulary, and encourage students to create their own mnemonics to personalize the process.

Advance and Graphic Organizers

Advance organizers provide an overview of new material and present students with organizational structures to help them link new content to what they already know (Luiten, Ames, & Ackerson, 1980).

Advance organizers can be provided orally or take the form of a unit or course outline, the table of contents in a textbook, or a visual concept map. Graphic organizers provide a visual, holistic representation of facts and concepts and their relationships within an organized frame. Teachers can use graphic organizers at the start of new instruction to activate prior knowledge (e.g., a KWL chart), as well as during instruction to help learners integrate new information and to encourage student predictions (e.g., a story-structure organizer). After instruction, they can use graphic organizers (e.g., a mind map) to summarize learning, encourage elaboration, help organize ideas for writing, provide a structure for review, and assess the degree of student understanding.

Note: We distinguish organizers that are prepared by the teacher and help with knowledge and skill acquisition from graphic organizers that are student constructed and require active meaning making. These latter types of organizers are described later in the chapter.

Process Guides

For learning a skill, a step-by-step guide can be helpful. Such how-to guides are especially useful for breaking down complex or multistep skills into chunks that students can practice in the proper sequence. Today's learners have access to a profusion of apps and websites (e.g., www.youtube.com, www.kahnacademy.com) offering online tutorials that provide detailed multimedia directions for learning a wide variety of skills.

Mental Manipulation for Meaning Making

Rote memory is considered successful if the learner can produce the "correct" response to a question or stimulus. However, even though memories may be strong in terms of isolated facts, skills, or procedures held within their individual neural circuits, the quantity and accuracy of rote memories will not ensure that students have a deep understanding of the content material. If students learn factual information only in response to specific stimuli, they will only be able to retrieve it with those same prompts. Without further mental manipulation, students will not develop the extended neural networks linking factual knowledge with the conceptual "big ideas" that are the basis for understanding and transfer. In this section we describe a number of effective teaching strategies that will help students mentally manipulate new learning through active engagement and recognition of relationships. This engagement and recognition enables neuroplasticity to work its magic, consolidating the short-term memories into enduring understanding for long-term memory networks with transferrable knowledge.

Teaching for understanding must push beyond instruction for acquisition of foundational knowledge and skills. Indeed, a fundamental contention of UbD is that a teacher's job is not to simply cover content and hope that it sticks; it is to enable learners to construct meaning about important ideas and processes so that they will be able to effectively transfer their learning to new situations. When understanding is a goal, the teacher's role expands from being primarily a dispenser of information or a modeler of a skill (the "sage on the stage") to a facilitator of meaning making and a coach for transfer (a "guide on the side"). The *M* and *T* of AMT require that we carefully consider the teaching and learning experiences that will help learners come to understand and equip them for autonomous transfer.

Understanding is not something that teachers can transmit simply by telling. Although they can directly teach facts and procedures, understanding must be constructed in the mind of the learner. In other words, the brain must *do* something with knowledge if it is to become incorporated into extended-memory networks of core concepts that can be applied in meaningful and novel ways. It is through the mental manipulation of content involving the brain's executive functions (higher-order thinking processes) that students construct and expand the neural networks needed for understanding.

We have identified six specific and practical teaching techniques that teachers can use to engage the brain's executive functions to support student meaning making: (1) summarize and synthesize, (2) compare and categorize, (3) symbolize, (4) predict, (5) use graphic organizers, and (6) pose essential questions with follow-up probes. Let's look at each of these in turn.

Summarize and Synthesize

Researchers have concluded that having students summarize enhances their understanding of academic content (Haystead & Marzano, 2009). To summarize information concisely, students must apply their executive functions to *analyze* a quantity of information, *prioritize* it to determine what is most important, and *synthesize* it to determine the essential gist. This active mental manipulation deepens understanding and cements learning into long-term memory. Here are a few examples of ways to get students to summarize and synthesize:

- Paired reading—Have students summarize key passages with partners or in small groups.
- Tweet—Have students create a tweet as a concise summary (on a device or on paper that has the 280 characters that are allowed in a tweet). Students can post their tweets on a class wiki or on a learning platform such as Moodle, with either their names or instructor-provided codes. Classmates benefit by reading each other's summaries as an additional way to understand the material as they build their own skills of analysis and synthesis.
- Study guide—Learners can develop a study guide (or a quick summary) of a new chapter for a student who has been absent.
- *Dend-writes*—As described in Chapter 4, *dend-writes* are so named to remind students that with mental manipulation they are constructing dendrites for enduring memory. Dend-writes can be used throughout instruction during periodic brain breaks, as exit cards before students leave class, or as homework. Here are examples of dend-write prompts:
  - *Write about how today's lesson reminded you of something you already know.*
  - *What is the one thing you'd like to remember about today's lesson?*
  - *How does something you learned today relate to something in your life?*
  - *Write about something that made you wonder or that surprised you.*
  - *What do you predict you will learn next in class?*
  - *How could you (or someone in a profession) use this knowledge?*
  - *Write about something you are confused about or found difficult.*
  - *Write about what you understood today that you haven't understood before.*
  - *Write to tell absent classmates what they missed in today's lesson.*

Compare and Categorize

A meta-analysis of instructional practices found that having students engage in comparative thinking has one of the greatest effects on student achievement of any instructional technique (Marzano, Pickering, & Pollock, 2001). This conclusion makes sense neurologically, because we know that one of the prime directives of the brain is to seek recognizable patterns in new sensory input, and after linking the new to the known in short-term memory, its system of storing, extending, and retrieving memory through pattern linkage is the basis for long-term, transferrable memory.

Recall that the brain has evolved toward efficiency and selective preferences to seek *patterns* and *pleasure.* The brain's system of pattern (relational) construction, retrieval, and expansion of memories lets us interpret the meaning of the many diverse pieces of sensory input received by the brain and guides our responses to that input.

To survive and thrive, animals need to collect information from and interpret their environments. The brain perceives and interprets new sensory information by associations to existing knowledge about what has previously been seen, heard, smelled, touched, tasted, and otherwise received through the senses. The brain uses previously stored data to predict the correct response to new stimuli with similar sensory representations.

For example, based on frequent links between a howl and a predatory wolf, our fox's brain might establish a memory pattern. The memory would result from frequent repetition of the pattern of howls and wolf attacks to other foxes in the vicinity. Therefore, the fox might predict that he should seek shelter or run on hearing that type of howl.

The brain constructs and expands learning into memory circuits through pattern recognition. As discussed earlier, after information passes through the amygdala en route to the upper brain, it enters the hippocampus, where short-term memories are formed. Successful construction of short-term memory occurs when sensory information is brought to the hippocampus and related to prior knowledge activated from storage. Once new information enters the hippocampus, it must connect with related information if it is to be encoded into short-term memory and ultimately retained as long-term memory.

Pattern recognition allows us to drive familiar routes without following specific verbal or written instructions each time. Pattern activation is how we can identify the name of or correctly "predict" most of the upcoming words of a familiar song after hearing the first few bars of music. As our brain's patterning systems become more efficient and the information stored in relational patterns (categories) becomes more accurate, we have more accessible information for making successful predictions, which affects our responses to questions and our behavior choices in novel situations. As patterns increase in content, through experience, predictions related to everything from literacy to responding to emotional cues are increasingly accurate and precise.

Pattern linking in the hippocampus is a collaborative interaction involving input from the executive function networks in the prefrontal cortex. When the brain has a goal in mind, attention is directed to search the environment for sensory input related to the goal and seek out related prior knowledge from memory storage to hook onto (integrate) the new information.

Correlating the neuroscience to the classroom provides a reminder that even when teachers feel the learning goals are clear, they should check in with students periodically and ask them, "Why should you learn this?" If students are connected to the goals by relevance and interest, they have the potential for greater success in activating related patterns in prior knowledge throughout their learning.

As the brain stores information in the related patterns of concepts and these neural networks are repeatedly activated by review and application, the brain constructs and expands its memory networks (Marshall & Bredy, 2016). By understanding how the brain works and using strategies that are compatible with brain research, students gain greater ability and motivation to add new learning—to construct more accurate and expanded networks of related information (concepts) that guide better and better predictions. These are the students who will be best prepared to achieve the life goals they choose. They will have an accumulation of learning stored efficiently in concept networks to make accurate choices, hypotheses, and analyses more frequently. They will use their expanded intelligence far beyond animals' use of better prediction for better survival.

One fundamental way that the brain forms patterns is by looking for similarities and differences as a basis for forming conceptual categories. A well-established teaching technique, known as *concept attainment,* mimics the mental process by which the human brain forms concepts. The educational application of this idea is grounded in the psychological research of Jerome Bruner (1973), who concluded that humans naturally group information into categories based on common characteristics as a means of making sense of a complex environment. Here's the basic theory: Students come to understand a new concept by forming a mental prototype based on an example of the concept provided by a teacher, a book, or another source; then by analyzing additional cases as either examples or nonexamples of the concept, students sharpen their understanding of the concept.

The concept-attainment instructional technique reflects this theory by actively engaging students in constructing a personal conception of a new concept through an inductive process of comparing examples and nonexamples, analyzing key attributes, and forming concept categories. In essence, students must construct, and then test, their theory about the essential attributes of a concept. Here is one version (Silver, Strong, & Perini, 2007) of the concept-attainment technique for developing and deepening student understanding:

1. Identify a concept with clear critical attributes (e.g., impressionist paintings, linear equations).
2. Present students with examples of the concept, contrasted with nonexamples.
3. Ask students to compare the two sets and try to determine what all the positive examples (+) have in common and what distinguishes them from the nonexamples (–). (In other words, students must develop a conceptual definition of critical attributes.)
4. Then, show additional examples that are positive (+) and negative (–) that students can use to test and refine their initial lists of attributes.
5. As a whole class, review the positive and negative examples and generate a final set of critical attributes.
6. Finally, ask students to demonstrate their understanding of the concept (e.g., by coming up with new examples of the concept on their own or applying the concept in a task).

This technique is universal; teachers can use it with learners from preschoolers to adults, across all disciplines, whenever they want learners to actively construct meaning.

Another applicable technique for meaning making involves comparison, categorizing, and inferencing. The following example was developed by Barry Beyer (1997) for a social studies lesson as part of a unit on the topic of westward expansion. Students are presented with a list of words associated with pioneer life in the Midwest in the 1800s. They are then asked: *What can you infer about pioneer life by examining these commonly used words from this era?* Here is the list of words:

hearthstone	gopher	woodchuck	bonnet	squall
mica	petticoat	tumbleweed	pitchfork	lantern
windmill	zinnias	ladder	biscuit	kettle
axe	overalls	wagon	hammer	saw
whicker	paddock	nasturtiums	horses	meadowlark
hailstones	harvest	churn	suspenders	plow

Students work in pairs to study the words (including looking up definitions for unfamiliar ones), and then begin to group them into categories. Their categorization leads to making inferences about the nature of pioneer life—for example, physical labor, farming, influenced by weather, practical (versus fashionable) clothing, no "modern" conveniences, not much leisure time.

This categorizing technique can be used in many subject areas and offers a constructivist alternative to simply having students memorize academic vocabulary. Another straightforward application of categorization is to have students create their own systems of categorizing the content of a unit, and to explain their thinking as they compare and classify information and key concepts.

Symbolize

Understanding is greatly facilitated when students have the opportunity to symbolize new learning in different representations—to translate acquired knowledge into different forms, such as developing a PowerPoint presentation, creating a board game, designing a museum display, and translating the learning into art forms by making a video, skit, rap, or drawing. Such mental manipulation helps to build, extend, and connect neural networks, which results in deeper learning.

Another way to help students symbolize new information is to have them create physical models to illustrate abstract concepts. Models can be created in a variety of ways, including cutting circles into pizza slices to illustrate fractions, using cereal and dried fruit pieces to create a 3-D model of a cell, or having students use their fists to represent the different lobes of the brain.

Analogies (similes and metaphors) offer a more abstract form of symbolic manipulation. An analogy compares the similarities of two concepts and helps to explain one thing by linking it to another, more familiar one. Having students create analogies activates the brain's pattern matching as they recognize and link the new to the known. Here's a basic analogy prompt and example:

> ____________ *is like* ______________ *because* ______________.
>
> A mystery story *is like* a roller coaster *because* the plot takes you up and down and all around.

When students create their own analogies, they are personalizing the connections to memory patterns that are already strong in their brains. Additionally, student-generated analogies can serve as formative assessments by revealing a student's degree of understanding of new, and especially abstract, material. For example, a flawed analogy may indicate that the student who developed it harbors a misconception that needs to be corrected.

Predict

A prediction is a forecast of future probabilities based on pattern recognition. The brain's ability to make sound predictions is fundamental to survival. As we discussed earlier, the brain rewards successful prediction through its pleasure drug (dopamine), thus reinforcing underlying patterns. The holding center for dopamine, the nucleus accumbens (NAc), is found near the amygdala. The nucleus accumbens constantly releases a small, steady stream of dopamine into the area of the prefrontal cortex where prior knowledge, in the form of memories, is brought when making a prediction. When feedback confirms that a prediction is correct, the NAc releases an extra supply of dopamine into this region of the prefrontal cortex, and the brain experiences an increase in positive feelings (Richard et al., 2013).

The positive pleasure response to the release of dopamine strengthens the neural memory networks that were activated and used to make that successful prediction. This strengthening increases the likelihood that the same response will be made when a similar question or choice comes up again. Neurologically, this system promotes animal survival by rewarding good choices so that they are remembered and repeated.

Anyone who has experienced the joy of bedtime reading to toddlers knows that it is not uncommon for young children to request the *same* story, night after night. As the story becomes familiar, the kids begin to anticipate what will happen on the next page. Then, when they correctly predict what will happen next, the brain rewards their prediction through a release of dopamine, leading to feelings of satisfaction and pleasure.

Indeed, this dopamine-reward response is particularly generous in young children. Although it soon evolves to responding to real predictions (that is, choices or answers that are *not* known for sure), during the bedtime-story years this prediction-reward response is activated even when the child knows with great certainty what is on the next page. Fast-forward to the school years. Teachers can productively harness the prediction power of the dopamine-reward cycle to engage attention, sustain motivation, and promote durable memory.

When learners are curious about something, they are in a perfect mental state to want to make predictions. Prediction activates the brain's instinctual need to know the result of one's choice, decision, action, or answer. When teachers provide opportunities for students to make predictions about the relationship of the curious sensory input or other novelty to the lesson, the students will seek information to help them make correct predictions, and they will remain attentive as the brain seeks to find out if the prediction is correct.

Teachers can use "hooks"—such as a surprise, an anomaly, or a provocative question—to spark students' curiosity, setting the stage for having the students make predictions that will prompt their brains to attend to the lesson as it becomes a source of clues to guide or adjust their correct predictions. After their curiosity is provoked, students will sustain attention if they are asked to predict what the curiosity-stimulating sight, sound, object, statement, picture, or question has to do with the lesson.

Although predictions are a natural way to capitalize on curiosity at the start of a new unit or lesson, predictions can (and should) be used throughout a unit of study to keep students' brains engaged. For example, in a science lesson for 1st graders, the teacher asks the children to predict which objects will float and which will sink in a tub of water; a middle school language arts teacher asks students to predict how a literary character will respond to a challenge presented in the opening chapter of a novel; a high school psychology teacher asks his class to predict (in advance) the results of a schoolwide student survey that they are about to give. In all cases, students are eager to find out if their predictions are correct. Check out this Pinterest website for dozens of additional ideas and tools for using prediction in the classroom: www.pinterest.com/explore/making-predictions.

Note: It is important that *all* students make predictions—for example, by writing their predictions on an individual whiteboard, giving a thumbs-up or thumbs-down signal, or using an electronic student-response clicker or smartphone app. With multiple opportunities to predict and multiple possible correct predictions, the combination of curiosity and prediction in the classroom will create a learning environment in which students sustain their focus because they intrinsically want to know what the teacher is going to teach.

Use Graphic Organizers for Constructing Meaning

We referenced graphic organizers earlier in the chapter as tools to help students acquire new information. Often such advance and graphic organizers are predeveloped—for example, a concept map for statistics; a story-structure organizer that lays out the components of a story (characters, setting, narrative arc, and ending); a Venn diagram where the dimensions for a comparison between mammals and reptiles are given to the students. The structure of such organizers provides external pattern scaffolding. They clearly aid assimilation of new information by making the invisible visible. However, such predeveloped organizers do not require significant mental manipulation by the learner.

Having students create their own organizers engages them in actively constructing meaning on their own. For example, learners can develop their own concept maps to show the hierarchy and interconnections among key ideas being learned in a unit. They can develop their own structure maps for organizing an argument. They can develop a comparison matrix by identifying the salient dimensions of different political philosophies to be compared.

Understanding is deepened as students take control of their personal meaning construction by creating their own organizers and related learning strategies. In doing so, they are exercising and developing the executive function skill sets needed for independent, lifelong learning. Indeed, the often-cited goal of college and career readiness demands that students develop the capacity to function autonomously, rather than always being directed and spoon-fed by teachers.

Pose Essential Questions with Follow-up Probes

For centuries, Socratic questioning has proven to be a robust method for engaging student thinking, promoting discussion, fueling debate, and deepening understanding. As a cornerstone of UbD, teachers are advised to frame the content they are teaching through open-ended essential questions designed to promote sustained inquiry and meaning making by learners (McTighe & Wiggins, 2013). Essential questions are linked to the larger, transferable ideas and processes that we want our students to come to understand. Unlike classroom questions that have a single correct answer, you can't search the internet for the answers to essential questions! Because there is rarely a final, conclusive "answer," the questions are meant to be explored over time, and students are expected to support their responses while considering alternate ideas and varied points of view. Often an essential question will open the door for more student questions, thus encouraging an inquiry-based classroom. Here are a few examples of such questions:

- *How do the arts reflect, as well as shape, culture?*
- *How does where we live influence how we live?*
- *Whose "story" is this?*
- *What do effective problem solvers do when they get stuck?*
- *How should we validate a scientific claim?*
- *Who wins and who loses when technologies change?*
- *How do I know what to believe in what I read, hear, and view?*
- *Is aging a disease?*

When posing essential questions, teachers assume a Socratic stance and use follow-up probes in response to students' responses; for example, *Why? What do you mean by ________? Can you give me an example or analogy to explain that? Is there another perspective on this? What's your evidence? Might there be different ways of thinking about this? What would you say to someone who disagrees with you?*

We recommend that teachers post their essential questions prominently in the classroom and leave them up throughout a unit of study, and in some cases, for the entire school year. The posted questions send signals that these are important inquiries, that we will keep considering them, and that the students' job is to make meaning.

More Methods for Meaning Making

In addition to these six specific techniques, a number of generalized teaching and learning methods require active meaning making by learners. Here are a few examples:

- Inquiry-oriented approaches (e.g., the 5 *E*s—engage, explore, explain, elaborate, evaluate—of investigative science)
- Project- and problem-based learning
- Socratic seminar
- Cooperative learning
- Simulation and role-plays
- Design thinking (e.g., using "maker spaces," where students can create tangible products)
- Reciprocal teaching
- Reading and writing across the curriculum

A detailed description of each of these (and related) teaching techniques and instructional methods is beyond the scope of this book but the following websites provide more information about any of the particular strategies:

- http://instructionalstrategies.org
- www.fortheteachers.org/instructional_strategies
- www.marzanoresearch.com/research/database/data

Chapter Understandings

- Successful mental manipulations enable students to interact with knowledge in ways that arouse their interest, activate positive emotions, connect the new information with their past experiences, and emphasize relationships of new memory to established neural networks. With mental manipulation, a new memory that might otherwise be forgotten is linked to and retained in a more durable memory storage pathway.
- Through regular opportunities to summarize and synthesize, compare and categorize, symbolize, generate and test predictions, use graphic organizers to construct meaning, and explore open-ended, essential questions, newly encoded short-term neural connections

holding bits of facts or procedures undergo the cellular changes of neuroplasticity and link into stronger and more durable long-term memory networks. By engaging students in these processes of active meaning making, teachers equip learners with the deeper learning needed for transfer.

Questions and Answers

How can teachers help students understand neuroplasticity and their own brainpower to help them sustain effort and persevere through setbacks?

Here are some ways we've explained their brainpowers to learners. You are right when you think school gets harder each year as you have more to learn and more homework to do. Fortunately, your brain is ready for the challenge. This is your brainpower of neuroplasticity. The way neuroplasticity works is similar to how exercise builds your muscle bulk. Each time a brain network (such as holding a memory or controlling a skill) is activated through review, practice, and application, the stronger and more powerful it becomes.

During your school years, your brain's neuroplasticity is at its peak. At no other time in your life will your memory circuits be so wired to hold or apply what you learn, apply, review, and practice.

Practice makes permanent. What happened in your brain as you progress from not knowing how to build with LEGO bricks, read, play the guitar, or ride a bike to when you can do these things? Why don't you forget these skills after not doing them for a while? The reason is that each time you practice or apply new knowledge or skills, learning became stronger due to your brain's neuroplasticity.

Everything you start to learn is stored in weak memory circuits. These circuits are needed to connect many brain cells, each holding a tiny bit of the memory. Think of each brain cell as a knot in a rope. Without the pieces of rope between the knots, there would just be a pile of knots. When memories are first formed as you are learning something new, the connections between the brain cells are weak—like thin string. That means the memory is not easy to remember and can be forgotten.

But every time you activate a memory (such as by practicing your keyboarding, soccer kick, multiplication tables, or speaking in a new language), an electrical current travels from one neuron to the next in the circuit. This electrical current triggers the neuroplastic response. This means the connections between your brain cells become thicker, last longer, and allow you to recall the memory or repeat the skill more and more easily.

Ultimately, with enough repeated use of these circuits, memories and skills become so strongly connected that they are automatic and don't dissolve before the final exam or during summer break. And there seems to be no limit in terms of the strength or amount of information you can hold in the neural networks you construct through neuroplasticity.

Why are some types of mental manipulation more powerful for memory and understanding than others? How can teachers maximize deep and enduring learning for their students?

Not all types of study or review activate short-term memories equally. Doing something active with your initial learnings will transform fragile new learning into solidly wired long-term memory. Teachers can help learners build stronger and more durable long-term memory networks by engaging them in meaning-making activities (e.g., by having them summarize, synthesize, compare and categorize, symbolize, construct meaning, and explore open-ended, essential questions). These active mental manipulations trigger related memory networks to come online to bolster the new learning. As a result of neuroplasticity, these previously unconnected networks become linked, such that subsequent activation of one part of the expanded network can retrieve the knowledge in its new partner, and both are reinforced when either is activated in the future.

Existing memory networks can be used to integrate new information. Most students have a strong foundation of memories about stories from books or movies. These early childhood memories have established a story framework—a beginning (e.g., once upon a time…), a set of characters, a problem, and a resolution or ending (e.g., happily ever after). Students' encoded knowledge of story patterns provides a template by which their brains can organize and connect new learning. For example, students studying the circulatory system or a historical period are able to symbolize and synthesize the new information into a durable memorable pattern associated with childhood stories. Here's an example:

Beginning: *Once upon a time*... the colonists living in what is now the United States were under the rule of the king who ruled Great Britain.

Problem: The British were making the colonists pay high taxes on things they needed but did not allow them to have any say in the laws they had to follow.

Resolution: The colonists protested and eventually fought a war that forced the British to give them independence.

Ending: The rebellious colonists won their struggle for independence and a new nation was born. We celebrate that momentous achievement each year on the Fourth of July.

In short, teachers who provide regular opportunities for students to connect new information to previously stored knowledge—and engage them in active meaning making through mental manipulation—help construct the durable neural networks needed for deep knowledge transfer.

6

Brain-Sensitive Teaching Using the WHERETO Model

The best teachers do not just show up at school and wing it. They carefully plan their lessons to be both engaging and effective for their students. To assist with instructional planning, Wiggins and McTighe (2004) developed the acronym WHERETO. This acronym refers to important elements of instructional design, reflects best pedagogical practices, and aligns with the neuroscience of learning. In this chapter we'll explain the WHERETO elements in their support of effective and engaging teaching for deep learning.

The WHERETO Elements

We'll begin with a brief look at the basic idea behind each letter of the acronym and frame the key questions to consider for instructional planning. Next, we'll explore each of the WHERETO elements in detail, offering specific teaching suggestions illustrated through classroom examples.

W—Ensure that all students understand the goals of a new unit; that is, ***where*** the unit is headed, ***why*** the new learning will be important and useful, and ***what*** is expected of the learners. Consider these questions: *How will I help students know where we are headed in this unit (that is, establish unit goals)? How can I connect this new learning to past learnings and experiences? How can I help them see purpose and relevance of the new learning? How will I preview how their learning will be assessed (that is, determine assessments and success criteria)?*

H—***Hook*** students to capture their attention in the beginning and ***hold*** their interest throughout the unit. Consider these questions: *What* *interesting and thought-provoking hook could I use to engage my students? How can I tap into the brain's natural curiosity to hook learners around this new topic? How might I sustain students' interest over time, especially when the going gets difficult?*

E—Determine what learning experiences will ***equip*** students with the necessary knowledge, skills, and understandings so that they will be prepared to meet performance goals. Consider these questions: *What learning experiences will help students acquire and retain foundational information and basic skills? How will I engage learners in actively making meaning of the big ideas and essential questions? How will I equip students to be able to transfer their learning in performance tasks?*

R—Provide students with opportunities to ***rethink*** big ideas and ***revise*** their work based on formative feedback. Consider these questions: *How can I deepen students' understandings by guiding them to rethink their comprehension of important ideas? How will I provide helpful feedback to help students improve their products and performances through revision?*

E—Build in opportunities for students to monitor and ***evaluate*** their progress along the way. Consider this question: *How can I encourage students' metacognition by monitoring and self-evaluating their performance?*

T—***Tailor*** the unit to differentiate and personalize the learning plan so that each student works toward an appropriate and achievable challenge. Consider this question: *How could I encourage students' metacognition by monitoring and self-evaluating their performance?*

O—***Organize*** and sequence the unit's lessons to maximize student engagement and effectiveness. Consider these questions: *What lesson sequence can make learning most interesting for students? In what ways can I make the lessons flow in a brain-friendly manner?*

Let's now explore connections between these elements and brain-centered learning.

Establishing the Where, Why, and What: The *W* in WHERETO

Research and experience underscore common sense: learners are more likely to focus their efforts when there is a clear and worthwhile learning goal. As noted in Chapter 1, the brain is goal oriented. If a learning goal is unclear or irrelevant to students, it is unlikely that they will maintain attention or try their best. The *W* in WHERETO simply reminds us that as teachers we must make the learning goals evident to students and help them recognize that the goal is both meaningful and attainable. Moreover, we also want students to understand what goal achievement looks like—in other words, how their learning will be assessed and by what success criteria it will be judged.

Here's our challenge to teachers: Can you make your learning goals as clear to students as those of a video game? Wiggins and McTighe (2011) offer practical actions that teachers can take to help students know where a new unit is going, why it is important to learn, and how their learning will be assessed.

- Directly state the learning goals at the beginning of the unit, and link these to longer-term year or course goals.
- Show how the work of daily lessons is linked to unit goals and will help prepare students for upcoming performance tasks.
- Help students see the rationale and relevance for targeted learning. For example, identify people and places beyond the classroom where this knowledge and these skills are applied.
- Invite students to generate questions about the unit topic (the *W* in KWL).
- Ask students to identify personal learning goals.
- Post and discuss essential questions at the start of the unit. Connect to the essential questions in daily lessons.
- Present the culminating performance task requirements.
- Involve students in identifying success criteria for the upcoming work.
- Review scoring rubrics.
- Show models or exemplars for expected products or performances.

So, how will you know if students have goal clarity? If they do, they should be able to answer these kinds of questions as the unit unfolds:

- *What will I be learning in this unit?*
- *What will I better understand by the end of the unit?*
- *Why do I need to learn this? Who uses this learning outside school?*
- *What knowledge and skill will I need to perform well?*
- *How will my learning and proficiency be judged?*
- *What makes a successful demonstration of my learning?*
- *How does today's lesson relate to what we did previously?*

Capturing and Holding Students' Attention: The *H* in WHERETO

Anyone who has taught in a preK–12 classroom for more than a few weeks recognizes that a brilliantly planned lesson or unit will not deliver on its promise if students are not engaged by the topic or attentive to the instruction. In other words, one of the first jobs of a teacher is to excite students about the prospects of new learning and focus their attention accordingly. In previous chapters, we discussed the value of creating authentic performance tasks to help students see the relevance of new learning. By presenting the tasks and associated rubrics at the beginning of a unit of instruction, we provide learners with clear performance goals and an understanding of the criteria needed for a successful performance. Note that by attending to the *W* in WHERETO, teachers can address the brain's need for clear and worthy goals cast in terms of an achievable challenge.

How, then, can we capture their attention at the start of a new learning trajectory? Before looking at specific attention-getting teaching strategies, let's revisit the fox we introduced in Chapter 1 to better understand the neurological underpinnings of attention. Recall that the brain has evolved adaptations that promote survival. We've learned that the human reticular activating system (RAS) is very similar to the RAS of other mammals in that it prioritizes its attention on those stimuli most critical to survival in an unpredictable environment. This process exists in the young brain as well as in more mature brains. However, as predatory wolves are rarely a threat in today's classrooms and students do not have to chase down lunch to survive, the sensory-intake priorities of what might be perceived as a threat by animals in unpredictable environments have not really kept pace with human evolutionary development. Nevertheless, to consider the priority given by the RAS to perceived threat, we can think of a student's RAS as responding much like that of our fox. For example, when the fox comes out of its den in the morning, there is likely to be one or more changes in the expected pattern in its environment. The howling of a predatory wolf and a rabbit running by could be two novel events—changes in the expected daily pattern. Because it represents danger, the howling of the wolf would get first priority; only when that sound is gone would the RAS grant entry to the nonthreatening changes in sensory input, such as the sights and sounds of the running rabbit. Assuming that students feel physically and psychologically safe in a classroom (something we address in Chapter 7), teachers can then take advantage of the brain's attention filter and its proclivity for attending to new, unfamiliar, or unexpected stimuli.

One way to gain the brain's attention at the beginning of a unit or lesson is through a *hook* (the *H* in WHERETO). As just described, the brain's attention filter gives priority to sensory input that is unexpected—a change in the expected pattern. Teachers can hook students' attention by starting new learning with something novel or unexpected. This can include curious objects; surprise; provocative questions; humor; or a weird fact, an anomaly, a counterintuitive example, or a discrepant event that will be related to the lesson. These hooks not only capture attention, they also can *hold* it when students have opportunities to generate and revise predictions about how the hook links to the broader topic of instruction.

Over the years, teachers have developed ingenious ways of capturing students' attention; these fall into recognizable categories (Wiggins & McTighe, 2004). Figure 6.1 presents various types of hooks and includes examples.

Here are two considerations to keep in mind when using such attention-getting hooks: (1) the goal is not simply to gain gratuitous attention—the hook should link to the topic being taught; and (2) grabbing students' initial attention is valuable but insufficient. The longer-term goal is to also hold their attention over time. Although the introductory hook opens the door to student interest, the teacher's job is to keep them in the room!

As we've described, a prime motivator driving dedicated video gamers to engage and persevere is the brain's dopamine-reward response. Gamers receive a dopamine reward when they receive helpful feedback leading to incremental progress toward their goal and acknowledgment of their positive growth. Teachers can use the key features of popular video games as a guide to sustaining student attention and motivated effort over time. These features are (1) an appealing, personally relevant goal; (2) an individualized, achievable challenge (that is, incremental skills progression from easier to more challenging); (3) frequent feedback to inform needed improvements; and (4) acknowledgment of incremental progress toward the goal.

Increasing the personal relevance of information that must be learned promotes greater attention and sustained effort by learners.

Figure 6.1 Types of Hooks, with Examples

Type of Hook	Example
Prediction—Confront students with a situation and have them generate a prediction.	A kindergarten teacher shows her students a tall vertical cylinder filled with water and asks them to predict whether the water will fit into a shorter, wider container. Then she "tests" their predictions.
Oddity—Present students with a weird fact, an anomaly, a counterintuitive example, or a discrepant event.	A science teacher blows up a balloon, then slowly pierces one end with a sharpened wooden cooking skewer. To the amazement of students, the teacher pushes the skewer through the opposite side of the balloon without bursting it.
Provocative question—Engage students with a thought-provoking question linked to their experiences or interests.	At the start of a health unit on nutrition, a 7th grade teacher poses this question: *Can what you eat help prevent zits?*
Mystery—Present a list of clues to a "mystery" that students will try to solve.	A 3rd grade teacher shows students a paper bag in which she has hidden an object, describes a few characteristics, and invites students to ask only "yes/no" questions to narrow down options about what is in the bag.
Surprise—Break the normal classroom routine and get students' attention with an unexpected or surprising event.	At the beginning of a new unit on negative numbers, or on past tense in language, the teacher enters the room walking backward and then asks students to guess why.
Authentic problem or issue—Engage students with an authentic problem or an issue that is relevant to them.	At the start of a unit on persuasive writing, a middle school teacher shows a newspaper article about a school board proposal that would require students to wear school uniforms, then asks students to consider the pros and cons.
Emotional connection—Captivate students' attention with a sensitive play on their emotions.	A teary-eyed biology teacher tells a true story of a young relative who was saved from a life-threatening illness by a breakthrough in genetic engineering. The story introduces a unit on genetics.
Personalization—Allow students to select a personal learning goal (related to the unit topic), to have choices to pursue an interest within a unit topic, or to propose how they will demonstrate their learning.	A government teacher invites students to select an issue at the school, community, state, or national level and prepare a blog post in which they state their personal position on the issue.
Humor—Boost dopamine levels in the brain by providing a funny start to a lesson or unit.	A math teacher begins a unit on ratio and proportion by presenting funny caricatures. She then shows Da Vinci's *Vitruvian Man* to illustrate "idealized" proportions of the human body.

Accordingly, teachers are encouraged to cast academic goals in ways that students see as interesting and personally germane. Making content more relevant and interesting decreases the likelihood that students will become bored with the material or fail to see the purpose in learning it. By framing learning goals in terms of authentic performance tasks and allowing student choice, teachers help students see relevance and tap into personal interests.

When students understand that learning goals will be within their reach, they have more motivation to persevere with the diligent work and repeated practice needed to acquire foundational knowledge and skills. By providing differentiated instructional support and ongoing feedback, teachers help students recognize that academic goals are achievable. By acknowledging and celebrating incremental growth, teachers can leverage the pleasure of dopamine release to encourage continued sustained effort and cultivate a growth mindset.

Equipping Students: The First *E* in WHERETO

When we refer to "equipping students," we mean helping them to *acquire* targeted knowledge and skills and to *make meaning* of larger ideas, and preparing them to *transfer* their learning on authentic performance tasks—the AMT discussed in Chapter 5.

Rethinking and Revising: The *R* in WHERETO

It is unlikely that students will arrive at deep understandings about abstract ideas on the first encounter. As Wiggins and McTighe (2012) note,

> The development of students' understanding develops over time through *multiple* opportunities to consider (and reconsider) the key ideas of the unit. Similarly, the capacity to transfer learning to new situations typically requires practice, feedback, and revision over time—*not* a one-shot attempt. (p. 113)

Indeed, a fundamental premise of UbD is that coming to an understanding occurs over time, and that "big" ideas must be regularly explored and reconsidered to move from surface to deep conceptualization.

Similarly, learners rarely produce a perfect product or a stellar performance on their first try, which is why rethinking and revision is a critical part of any constructive process—for example, writing a narrative story, engineering a design, investigating phenomena, creating a work of art, or planning for a debate. From a neuroscience perspective, when students are guided to rethink and revise, the associated neural networks expand and their understandings deepen. Further, the processes of rethinking and revising engage important executive functions, such as critical analysis, judgment, attention to feedback, and cognitive flexibility.

Wiggins and McTighe (2004) offer specific ways that teachers can prompt and encourage students to rethink and refine their understanding of important ideas in a variety of ways, including

- Playing devil's advocate to challenge a held conception or belief.
- Revisiting an essential question with new examples.
- Asking students to consider new information or conduct further research.
- Presenting alternative and contradictory examples.
- Asking students to consider things from a different perspective.
- Challenging key assumptions.
- Asking students to imagine themselves as a different person (e.g., "Assume the role of . . .; Imagine that you were . . .").

When instruction is organized for students' self-construction of understanding with opportunities to revisit big ideas and work toward transfer goals, there is greater cross-brain activation of previously isolated memory circuits that are now being used together. These expanded cross-brain neural networks then become available for subsequent transfer beyond the contexts in which the information was initially learned.

Rethinking and revising also come into play in terms of using mistakes as opportunities to deepen understanding. We've emphasized the benefits of activating the release of dopamine to promote intrinsic satisfaction and foster sustained effort. Dopamine also plays a role in how the brain learns from mistakes. In new situations, when the brain is not certain of the correct response, the related prior memories, stored throughout the cerebral cortex, are activated to guide in making the best prediction as to how to interpret new sensory input, environmental cues, questions, or decisions. These related prior memories are sent to the prefrontal cortex and used to guide the prediction of the best response to the new situation, the solution to a problem, or the answer to a question.

When the brain makes an incorrect prediction—a mistake, an error, an unsuccessful attempt—the nucleus accumbens responds by withholding that steady stream of dopamine to the prefrontal cortex. The brain registers a decrease in dopamine and reacts to this reduction of pleasure by seeking information (corrective feedback or guidance) to help it make a correct prediction to meet the challenge and reverse the dip in dopamine (Kuo, Paulus, & Nitsche, 2008).

Let's return to what we've learned from the video game model. Consider that dedicated gamers persevere through frequent failures and mistakes. They sustain effort through setbacks because they have come to recognize the pattern—by remaining open to feedback, they receive information that helps them correct their mistakes or overcome their misunderstandings and move forward. The associated dopamine reward of achieving the challenge (reaching the next level in the game) reinforces this productive pattern and supports a growth mindset.

Contrary to the attitude of gamers, some students in classrooms consider mistakes as evidence of lesser intelligence and assume that they cannot meet at least some academic challenges. If this becomes a pattern, it contributes to a fixed mindset and a reluctance to put forth effort or take risks, in order to avoid failure and embarrassment. Yet we know that mistakes are part of learning and some risk taking is needed for growth.

Here are seven things that a teacher can do to help students use mistakes to improve:

- Explain that mistakes are an accepted part of the learning process.
- Let students know that mistakes will not be penalized in this classroom.
- Encourage learners to try new things, respond to essential questions, make predictions, attempt challenging problems, and take responsible risks; then praise their attempts.
- Dignify errors and mistakes; avoid put-downs.
- Provide ongoing feedback, including opportunities for sharing and peer reviews.
- Allocate time for additional review and practice and for revision and refinement of work.
- Highlight and celebrate improvement and growth.

By regularly incorporating such methods by design, teachers can cultivate growth mindsets while deepening students' understanding, increasing skill proficiency, and enhancing the quality of their performances.

Encouraging Self-Evaluation: The Second *E* in WHERETO

This *E* underscores the value of metacognition in effective learning. *Metacognition* refers to the awareness of, and control over, one's cognitive processes. It involves goal setting, frequent monitoring of progress, self-evaluation, and reflection by the learner. Researchers point out that metacognitive abilities do not emerge spontaneously for most students (Brown, 1985). And because metacognition often takes the form of an internal dialogue, many students may be unaware of its importance unless the processes are explicitly emphasized by teachers. Thus the teaching of metacognitive skills should be integrated into the curriculum, and teachers should signal the importance of such skills and cultivate them explicitly.

Students need instruction, guidance, and practice to help them learn how to apply effective self-monitoring strategies to academic tasks, and teachers can apply a "gradual release of responsibility" protocol (Fisher & Frey, 2016) to the teaching of these metacognitive skills. Here is a summary of this effective skill-development technique:

1. Focused instruction (*I do, you watch.*)
Teachers directly introduce the skill, describe its purpose, and model it for learners. For metacognitive skills, teachers can think aloud to demonstrate how they are self-evaluating their performance, making adjustments based on feedback, or setting a new learning goal.
2. Guided instruction and practice (*You do, I watch.*)
Teachers guide students in applying the skill to a simple, familiar task and provide feedback. Over time, students apply the skill to increasingly complex tasks (e.g., reading, problem solving, writing, research), while teachers gradually reduce their input and feedback.
3. Independent (transfer) application (*You do it alone.*)
Teachers turn over responsibility to the students to apply these skills on their own in a variety of situations.

As students learn and practice metacognitive strategies, they will gradually internalize and automate them, thereby opening space in working memory for additional procedures and strategies.

Tailoring Learning to the Students: The *T* in WHERETO

The most effective teachers do not focus only on teaching content; they are mindful of, and responsive to, the needs of the learners they serve. The *T* in WHERETO serves as a reminder to tailor (or differentiate) teaching to address student differences in background knowledge and experiences, skill levels, interests, talents, cultural orientation, and preferred ways of learning. Although differentiation is certainly not a new idea in education, the neuroscience of learning illuminates the brain-based underpinnings of the value of this practice.

Recall that in the video game model, the achievement of challenges—reaching the game's next level, solving the mystery, slaying the dragon—results in the release of dopamine, one of the brain's most powerful reinforcers of continued effort. Their achievement (and associated dopamine reward) is made possible because the game brings players in at a challenge level just a bit above their current skill level. Through practice and focused effort, players can achieve the next level. If the game was impossibly hard, most players would quickly become discouraged and quit playing. Conversely, if the game was too easy, there would be no challenge—and a challenge must be present for dopamine to be released.

Ideally then, teachers will know their students well enough so that they can adjust the level of challenge so that each learner can work on a learning task in the Goldilocks zone—that is, it's not too easy, not too hard. In other words, we want students' brains to recognize that each new step to their learning goal is *challenging* but *achievable* for them. Both factors are needed to engage students' effort and motivation in order to benefit from the dopamine-reward system.

The information needed to determine the proper challenge level comes in large part from the regular use of pre- and ongoing assessments, as described in Chapter 4. This information enables teachers to determine the knowledge, skill, and achievement levels of their students, and to adjust their assignments and performance tasks into achievable challenges for each. Once student needs are identified, teachers can tailor their instruction and assessments to find optimal levels of challenge without sacrificing unit goals. Here are some specific ideas:

- Present open-ended questions, activities, assignments, and assessments that enable students to give different but equally valid responses.
- Present information through various modalities (orally, visually, and in writing).
- Provide texts and other resources at varied reading levels and in students' primary languages.
- Use tiered activities at different levels of difficulty but focused on the same learning goals.
- Provide kinesthetic learners with options for hands-on work or role-plays.
- Use videos and demonstrations to supplement and support verbal explanations and lectures.
- Use texts with key portions highlighted.
- Provide organizers and scaffolds to guide note taking and reviews.
- Provide key vocabulary lists for reference.
- Use learning buddies to work with challenging texts or assignments.
- Establish flexible groupings to address differences in knowledge and skill gaps.
- Use concrete materials and examples when teaching abstract concepts.
- Provide detailed and highly structured task directions for learners who need it, while leaving the task more open for more capable and independent students.
- Use materials, applications, examples, illustrations reflecting both genders, and materials that connect content to students' cultures and communities.
- Allow students choices of products (visual, written, oral) for activities, assignments, and assessments (e.g., by using the GRASPS elements, described in Chapter 4).
- Offer teacher-led miniworkshops on needed skills at varied levels of complexity based on student needs.
- Use computer-based and online tutorials at the student's individual level of readiness for skill practice and enrichment.

- Provide tailored homework assignments to differentiate challenge level.
- When appropriate, allow students to choose whether they work alone or in groups.
- Provide interest centers to encourage further exploration of topics.
- Connect to students' interests by encouraging them to develop and pursue their own questions related to the topics being studied.
- Use the jigsaw cooperative strategy to allow students to specialize in aspects of a topic they find interesting and then "teach" others.
- Allow students to propose interest-based projects and independent studies related to the content being learned.

For a more detailed discussion of differentiation, see *Differentiated Instruction and Understanding by Design: Connecting Content and Kids* (Tomlinson & McTighe, 2006).

Although the call to tailor instruction to meet the achievable challenge needs of every student is admirable, it is simply not feasible to suggest that teachers individualize instruction for every learner at all times. Nonetheless, we encourage teachers to tailor their lessons and assessments in ways that are most manageable and likely to have the highest yield for the greatest number of learners. The opportunities teachers provide for choice and more personalized skill building also activate neural networks related to executive function in students' brains, supporting their increased capacity for self-directed learning. Moreover, students are likely to recognize a teacher's efforts to get to know them as individuals and appreciate their attempts at tailoring.

Organizing for Learning and Engagement: The *O* in WHERETO

The way learning is organized and sequenced can influence students' engagement and the ultimate effectiveness of their learning. The typical sequence of conventional lessons involves a linear, topic-by-topic or skill-by-skill progression. This pattern is especially evident when textbooks are followed page by page or when teachers attempt to cover each grade-level standard in the order in which they are presented in standards documents. However, the logic of how content knowledge is organized does not automatically align with how the brain best learns—especially if the goals are to develop understanding and transfer abilities.

How, then, should teachers think about the sequence of their lessons? We suggest two general alternatives to a content-covering sequence: (1) performance-based learning and (2) narrative structure. These two approaches to instructional sequence trigger ideas for a more engaging, and ultimately successful, learning plan. Let's consider each in terms of how the brain learns.

Performance-based learning is developed as a result of attempting to solve complex problems, explore real issues and reach decisions, analyze real/simulated cases, or produce a genuine product or performance. Examples include *project/problem-based learning;* the *case method,* as applied in law, business, and medicine; *immersion,* as in language learning; and the *whole-part-whole* approach applied in the arts and athletics. Research in cognitive psychology supports the idea that when students have opportunities to design and conduct investigations and then evaluate their proposed solutions to real and personally relevant problems, they can construct greater problem-solving skills, understanding, learning, and memory (Finkelstein, Hanson, Huang, Hirschman, & Huang, 2010).

In performance-based learning, the learner knows the goal from the start—for example, solving a problem, finding an answer through inquiry, or achieving a desired performance. The particular skills and strategies needed for effective performance (the "pieces") are learned and practiced with constant feedback and the whole in mind. This is not an accretion (brick-by-brick) approach to constructing knowledge. Rather, it reflects backward design from successful performance. Note that in all of the approaches to performance-based learning, the needed knowledge and skills are developed *in the context of* preparing for meaningful performance. Accordingly, instruction is delivered (and sought by students) when there is a *need* to know. In other words, the sequence of teaching and learning is not prescribed in advance; rather it unfolds as learners strive to address a worthy challenge or achieve an authentic performance goal. For example, when learning a new language, students are immersed in a natural language environment within which they must learn to communicate, first by listening and speaking; later through reading and writing. The basics (vocabulary, syntax, rules of grammar) are then acquired in the context of working toward authentic communication.

This example from the United States Soccer Federation (n.d.), recommending a shift in coaching methods, makes the same point:

> When conducting training sessions, there needs to be a greater reliance on game-oriented training that is player centered and enables players to explore and arrive at solutions while they play. This is in contrast to the "coach-centered" training that has been the mainstay of coaching methodology over the years. . . . "Game-centered training" implies that the primary training environment is the game as opposed to training players in "drill" type environments. This is not to say that there is not a time for a more "direct" approach to coaching. At times, players need more guidance and direction as they are developing. However, if the goal is to develop creative players who have the abilities to solve problems, and interpret game situations by themselves, a "guided discovery" approach needs to be employed. This approach taps in to certain essentials that are always present within the team. Players want to play and enjoy playing the game first and foremost. Since the "game" is used in training, this allows for players to be comfortable with the pace, duration, and physical and mental demands that the game provides. The reason why the players play is because they enjoy the game. They have a passion for the game. This is where they find and express their joy and creativity. (p. 62)

A performance-oriented sequence that shifts the teaching and assessment of individual facts and skills in isolation toward a "game-centered" approach to learning honors how the brain learns naturally. As we've learned in correlation with neuroscience research, students need opportunities to sustain their engagement and allow their brain's neuroplasticity to construct the neural networks of expanded concept understanding. The opportunities provided in performance-based learning support the sustained engagement needed for students' brains to construct and expand these neural networks. This extended neural network creates new synapses and makes connections among previously isolated memories and concepts. Active and goal-directed learning promotes the activation of brain memory circuits that, through the neuroplastic response, expand their connections to other neural networks. This neural superstructure is the road to conceptual understanding and transfer.

Narrative Structure

An alternative approach to organizing and sequencing a unit takes a page out of a novel or a movie script. Think of the most compelling stories and films you've enjoyed over the years. They rarely follow a strict chronology whereby all the facts are laid out in order, one by one. Instead, you are immersed in the action immediately, confronted with a challenge, or faced with the perplexing facts of a mystery. Sometimes the story begins with a flashback; other times it starts with the ending. Although they may not have studied neuroscience, successful novelists and filmmakers nonetheless display a keen understanding of how the brain responds to narratives.

Earlier we referred to the pleasure of reading bedtime books to young children, which demonstrates one of the reasons why narratives are so compelling. During their childhoods, our daughters wanted the same books (e.g., *Goodnight Moon, The Cat in the Hat*) read to them again and again. Even after dozens of readings, they continued to excitedly predict what would be on the next page and take great pleasure in being right. That childhood desire, of wanting to hear books read aloud and repeatedly requesting those few whose stories they knew well enough to predict, encompasses powerful brain drives that become memory enhancers.

The experiences we have with narratives, starting as young children, establish supportive conditions in the brain for learning and remembering. A foundation arises, built upon emotional connections to the experience of being read to or told stories. In addition, the familiarity of the narrative pattern becomes a strong memory-holding template.

Although stories from childhood are generally associated with positive emotional experiences, they can also provide a link into the patterning system by which memories are stored. Our brains seek and store memories based on patterns (repeated relationships). This system facilitates our interpreting of the world (and all the new information and choices we make throughout each day) based on prior experiences. The narrative mental map is formed early and easily recognizable by its three-step progression:

1. Beginning (*Once upon a time…*)
2. Problem
3. Resolution (*… and they all lived happily ever after.*)

With time, that map expands to include narratives in which the ending is not "happily ever after."

Teachers can creatively harness the power of narrative to make learning more engaging and enduring. Here are some examples, in various subject areas.

Literature

Tell a story that previews key characters in a novel.

Charlie was about your age when he wanted to earn money with an after-school job. As you know, jobs for 15-year-olds are not easy to get. He finally got one at a fancy stationery store, like the ones we have on State Street. His task was to use the store's special glue to paste their fancy labels onto ink bottles. He was only paid for the good ones and had to do his bottles over and over because air bubbles would form under the label. One day, another boy, Bob, gave Charlie a piece of string and showed him how he could roll it over the label and get out the bubbles. You'll be interested to discover how Charles Dickens wrote about this boy, Bob Fagin, from the stationery shop in the book *Oliver Twist*, which you'll get to read next.

History

Use an account from a primary source to arouse student curiosity about a historical event.

"It started as a beautiful day here as we await their landing. After a spectacular first journey, the people on board were pleased by their success until they heard a disturbing sound that caused them to fear for their safe landing." Such an opening can be used to have students make predictions about the *who, what, when,* or *"how it turned out"* as a setup for exploring such topics as the *Hindenburg* disaster, the astronauts on *Apollo 13*, or the first flight of Orville and Wilbur Wright.

Use the "beginning, problem, resolution" structure to frame a major historical event.

Beginning: Once upon a time, the colonists living in what is now the United States were under the rule of the king who ruled Great Britain.

Problem: The British were making the colonists pay high taxes on things they needed and not allowing them to have any say in the laws they had to follow.
Resolution: The colonists protested and eventually fought a war that forced the British to give them independence. The struggle for independence led to victory for the colonists and ended with the birth of a new nation. We celebrate that momentous achievement each year on the Fourth of July.

Science

Make complex topics more understandable by creating "characters" that represent key elements.
To teach educators about the process of neuroplasticity, Judy created a narrative featuring Oli, an *oligodendrocyte* (a kind of cell involved in constructing memory). In the narrative, glial cells, particularly oligodendrocytes, travel to active axons and mediate the laying down of more layers of myelin. These cells link their branching arms to the axon and wrap their cytoplasm around it, thereby adding layers of myelin.

Have students translate their new learning into a story or dialogue.
The mental manipulations involved in creating a story help personalize new information, which increases memory linkages and enhances long-term retention. One student, for example, wrote an amusing story about a lonely piece of new information that entered the brain and felt very lost and sad until it found its "family" of related prior knowledge and linked with an extended network of long-term memory.

Mathematics

Use analogies to help students understand broad concepts.
Explore trends or patterns in economic markets using the analogy of a journey.

Tell a story that challenges students' presumptions and offers a "surprise" ending that makes students want to learn more.
Maria did her family jobs all week and loved waking up on Saturday and getting her allowance. When she turned 13, her parents offered her a choice. They said she could change to a

monthly allowance and receive $100 at the end of each month, or they would pay her one penny on the first day of the month and double the amount each following day for 30 days. Excited at the thought of getting $100 a month, Maria chose the first option. Which would you choose? (After students make their choices and then learn that the surprising result of the second option would be $5,368,709.12, they are ready to learn about *exponents*!)

Weaving learning into a story makes it more interesting, activates the brain's positive emotional state, and hooks the information into a strong memory template. Whether created by teachers or their students, the memory then becomes more durable as the learning follows the narrative pattern through sequences connected to a theme, time flow, or actions directed toward solving a problem or reaching a known goal. What's more, thinking about presenting content through narratives give teachers a chance to engage *their* creativity!

Chapter Understandings

This chapter introduced the acronym WHERETO and described its seven elements of effective and engaging instruction. We provided suggested questions for instructional planning, presented specific teaching suggestions, and made links to brain-based learning.

Questions and Answers

There are so many ideas related to WHERETO. How can a teacher possibly include all of these elements in every lesson?

We propose that the elements described in WHERETO should be considered when planning a unit—*not* for each individual lesson within it. Recognize that different WHERETO elements fit naturally at different points during a unit. For example, the *W* and *H* are typically addressed at or near the beginning of a unit, whereas the *R* comes later, and the second *E* would occur closer to the end.

We recommend that WHERETO should be considered aspirational (i.e., ideally, every unit would reflect all of these elements). Realistically, this would be quite a challenge, especially at the start. However, we think it is possible to begin with one or two elements and add additional ones to future units. Over time, we hope that you will find it easier and more natural to consider WHERETO when you plan and teach.

Could or should a principal use the WHERETO elements in a checklist when visiting classrooms for observations? What about for teacher evaluation?

Although we encourage the use of WHERETO to guide instructional planning, we caution against using it as a checklist or in terms of quotas (e.g., "I expect to see at least five of the WHERETO elements every time I visit your classroom"). Such an approach could engender teacher resentment and lead to a "minimum compliance" response (e.g., "I'll just throw in a 'hook' activity whenever the principal is visiting"). Rather, we prefer that administrators encourage the gradual introduction of the WHERETO elements without excessive pressure. For example, open a meeting (faculty, PLC, grade-level, department) by inviting teachers to share a specific example of how they used a WHERETO strategy and explain the results. Teachers are more likely to expand their instructional repertoires when they see others doing so and recognize that there are benefits to students.

The T *of WHERETO calls for differentiation. But I have too many students to tailor my learning plan for all of them. Is this really feasible?*

The call for tailoring does not mean that teachers must *individualize* for every learner at all times. Instead, we encourage you to tailor a unit plan in ways that are most manageable and likely to have the highest yield for the greatest number of learners. Try simple differentiating strategies, such as allowing students some choices in work process and product. As you get to know your students, you can also look for opportunities to integrate learners' interests into lessons and assessments whenever possible.

7

Creating a Brain-Friendly Classroom Climate

In this concluding chapter, we consider the significance of a classroom's climate in contributing to what the brain needs for optimal learning. We'll present a framework to help teachers consider the various social-emotional factors that can affect students' motivation, cause unhelpful stress, and impair their ability to think deeply about academic matters. We offer practical and proven interventions and strategies that can promote a positive climate, strengthen students' internal emotional resources, and minimize the influences of stressors that inhibit the brain's performance.

The Brain's Emotional Filter

Recall from Chapter 1 that sensory input, including information, must pass through the amygdala, the brain's emotional filter. In a neutral or positive emotional state, the amygdala directs information into and out of the prefrontal cortex, the highest cognitive and reflective region of the brain. In an interview, Mary Helen Immordino-Yang, a professor of education, psychology, and neuroscience, describes the centrality of emotions to cognition and learning:

> Experts traditionally thought, based on Descartes and other western philosophical traditions, that high-level cognition is purely rational and that emotion comes along and messes it up. What we're finding is that's not really the case. Instead, cognition happens *because of* emotions. There's really no such thing as a thought that doesn't have an emotion attached to it or that

> doesn't have an emotion that follows it.... All thinking is inherently emotional and cognitive all at once. (Varlas, 2018, p. 4)

We've learned that a positive emotional state can promote and sustain successful engagement, learning, and memory (Armenta, Fritz, & Lyubomirsky, 2017). We've also learned that connections to and from the prefrontal cortex are vital to input to and from the prefrontal cortex's executive function networks that direct more considered responses (top-down control) and make more extensive connections among stored memories (think *transfer*) (Berridge & Kringelbach, 2013). On the flip side, as noted in Chapter 1, when a mammal is in a state of stress—whether actual or perceived—new information does not move through the amygdala's filter and into the prefrontal cortex. Instead, the input goes to the lower, reactive brain, whose limited set of behavioral responses can be summarized as *fight, flight, or freeze*. In humans, this emotional response system operates much like that of mammals in the wild, where immediate, automatic responses are critical for survival. The human variations to the instinctive *fight, flight, or freeze* reactions include anger, acting out, withdrawing (zoning out or not doing assigned work), saying hurtful things, and risk taking, among others.

When learners are anxious, sad, frustrated, bored, hurt, or angry, the survival reactions can take over. Although valuable for survival in the wild, in classrooms these reflexive survival instincts can undermine the most carefully designed lessons. In fact, these primitive mammalian responses are what your students are likely to display when they are stressed by fear, lack of peer acceptance, repeated failures to achieve success in a task or a subject, or boredom. To be blunt, neither thought-provoking essential questions, authentic performance tasks, nor inspired teaching will realize their full intended effects if students are overly stressed, fearful, bored, or feeling rejected. Accordingly, effective teachers recognize that if they care about students' academic learning, they must also be attentive to the social and emotional factors that affect their learners.

The Teacher's Example

Not surprisingly, a teacher's attitude and emotional state can set the tone for a classroom. Two things that teachers can do to boost learners' emotional readiness for learning are to monitor their own moods and to project a sense of having fun in the classroom.

Monitor Your Moods

You might have noticed in classes you've been a part of that students' moods often seem to reflect the mood of the instructor. Teachers who are confident, are respectful of their students, are encouraging, and display a good sense of humor (without being sarcastic) can have a positive influence on students' moods. Conversely, when teachers are tired, stressed, or grumpy, learners may pick up and reflect those emotions back to the teacher and each other. One teacher remarked that she always tries to set a tone in her class as if she were celebrating a joyous event. She noted that by displaying positivity and an affirmative attitude even when she was tired or having a bad day, the kids would pick up the "vibe" and "feed off" her moods. We encourage you to regularly monitor your own temperament and be aware of the tone that you project.

Have Fun

Have you ever experienced a joyful classroom? You can recognize it by the facial expressions and body language of its inhabitants—both the young people and the adults. If your students see that you're happy and enjoying your job, they are much more apt to be happy and having fun as well. You'll notice their increased enthusiasm and responsiveness to instruction when you exude joy in teaching and find creative ways to connect students to their work. Indeed, the best teachers do more than just engage learners in a lesson; they sustain and renew a genuine joy in learning.

Social-Emotional Learning (SEL)

The growing recognition of the influence of emotions on learning has led to an increased interest in social-emotional learning (SEL) among educators. SEL initiatives are intended to help students become aware of their emotional states and recognize the stressors that can set their amygdala into overdrive. Such programs teach students ways to identify and express their feelings and introduce positive coping mechanisms for handling their stresses. These mechanisms include relaxation techniques, journaling, conflict resolution, and exercise. Some schools have introduced formal mindfulness programs (Srinivasan, 2014) to teach self-calming strategies and provide practice times for students to build habits such as focused breathing and calming visualizations.

Although certain factors—students' medical conditions, family dynamics, the heartbreaks of youth—are beyond educators' control, there are numerous ways in which teachers can influence the emotional climate of their classrooms and enhance students' motivation, attention, effort, and perseverance. Figure 7.1 presents a helpful organizer for identifying factors that influence students' emotional states and their willingness to focus effort on learning. We will use the categories shown in this graphic to describe significant social, emotional, and cognitive variables that affect learning and suggest actions teachers can take to augment student achievement—by design.

Figure 7.1 Variables Influencing Learners' Motivation and Effort

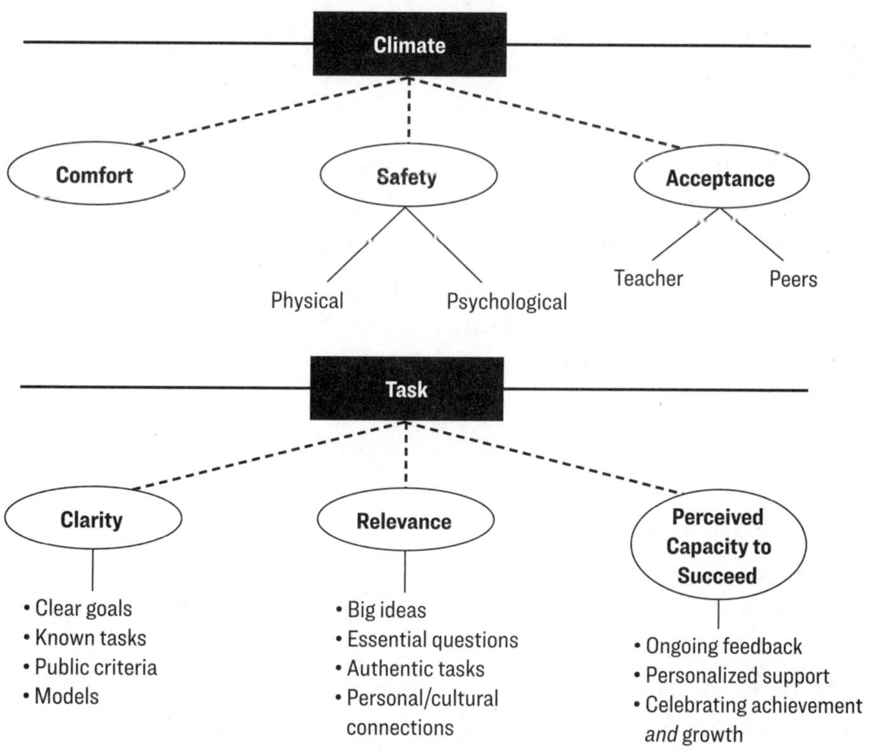

Climate Variables

The first broad category in Figure 7.1 identifies variables that affect school and classroom climate: *comfort, physical and psychological safety, teacher acceptance*, and *peer acceptance*. In the next sections we explore the effects of each of these on students' motivation and willingness to put forth effort.

Comfort

Not surprisingly, when learners are cold, hot, sleepy, or have been sitting too long, optimal learning is unlikely. Indeed, it is difficult to focus attention on lessons or homework when a person is uncomfortable. At a most basic level, sitting for long periods at school desks can be painful and make concentration difficult. Given this awareness, some schools have purchased standing desks and stools of varying heights so students can alternate between sitting and standing.

Alexis Wiggins, a high school teacher (and daughter of UbD co-creator Grant Wiggins), had a very personal reminder of the need to attend to comfort when she spent a day shadowing a student to get a sense of the school experience from a learner's perspective. Her experience was eye-opening. Here is an excerpt from her reflection:

> I could not believe how tired I was after the first day. I literally sat down the entire day, except for walking to and from classes. We forget as teachers, because we are on our feet a lot—in front of the board, pacing as we speak, circling around the room to check on student work, sitting, standing, kneeling down to chat with a student as she works through a difficult problem... we move a lot. But students move almost never. And never is exhausting. In every class for four long blocks, the expectation was for us to come in, take our seats, and sit down for the duration of the time. By the end of the day, I could not stop yawning and I was desperate to move or stretch. I couldn't believe how alert my host student was, because it took a lot of conscious effort for me not to get up and start doing jumping jacks in the middle of Science just to keep my mind and body from slipping into oblivion after so many hours of sitting passively. (Strauss, 2014b)

Alexis continues:

> If I could go back and change my classes now, I would immediately change the following three things:
>
> • stand for a mandatory stretch halfway through the class;
> • put a basketball hoop (for soft foam balls) on the back of my door and encourage kids to play in the first and final minutes of class; and
> • build in a hands-on, move-around activity into every single class day. Yes, we would sacrifice some content to do this—that's fine. I was so tired by the end of the day, I wasn't absorbing much of the content anyway, so I am not sure my previous method of making kids sit through hour-long, sit-down discussions of the texts was all that effective.

Although Alexis may not know the neuroscience, her instincts are correct. We recommend building in brain breaks, or "syn-*naps*," as a regular part of classroom instruction. Syn-*naps* are planned shifts in a learning activity that serve to return the amygdala from overdrive into the optimal state for successful flow of information. These shifts allow regions blocked by stress or high-intensity work to revitalize. Brain breaks switch activity to other brain networks, allowing the cognitive pathways to rest and recuperate. They should take place before fatigue, boredom, distraction, and inattention set in. Simply stretching, moving to a different part of the room, doing jumping jacks, or playing Simon Says will increase the blood flow and oxygen supply to the brain. In addition to physical movement, great mood-boosters that revitalize the brain include humor, listening to stories, singing songs, and interacting with peers.

Brain breaks do not require a disruption to the flow of learning. Use your learning goals to guide you in the selection of brain breaks that will enrich knowledge acquisition. Consider the following activities that not only involve movement but support multisensory learning and boost dopamine levels:

- Ball-Toss Review—Students toss a ball to one another as each student asks and answers questions to review a topic or summarizes key ideas remembered from a lesson.

- Pantomime—Students nonverbally act out the meaning of vocabulary words or content-area concepts.
- Snowball Toss—Each student writes a question on a piece of paper. The students then stand in two lines, or "teams," crumple their papers, and throw "snowballs" at the other team. They then select and unwrap the snowballs to try to answer the review questions.
- Four Corners—Each corner of the room is marked with the letters *A, B, C,* or *D*. Students answer teacher- and student-generated multiple-choice questions by moving to the corner designated as the choice they believe to be the correct answer.
- Bodies of Knowledge—Students move in ways that represent a biological, physical, or mathematical process. Alternately, they can mimic how a historical or literary character might interact in a given situation.
- Word Gallery—Numbered posters with a verbal or pictorial representation of a vocabulary word are placed around the classroom. Students then take a list of vocabulary words, walk around the room, and record the number of the poster that matches their words. Subsequently, students can add their own sentences or drawings to the wall charts. Playing music that students enjoy as they move around the classroom can make the activity even more dopamine enriching.

The frequency of brain breaks will vary depending on students' ages, but as a general rule, we recommend a 3- to 5-minute break after every 10 to 15 minutes of concentrated study for elementary school students, and after 20 to 30 minutes for middle and high school learners.

After just a few minutes, students' refreshed brains are ready to return to the next learning activity with a subdued amygdala and full supply of neurotransmitters. Both students and teachers will benefit from this restoration.

Physical and Psychological Safety

In a summary of research on effective schools, Lezotte (2001, p. 6) highlights the importance of a safe and orderly learning environment: "In the effective school there is an orderly, purposeful, business-like atmosphere which is free from the threat of physical harm. The school climate is not oppressive and is conducive to teaching and learning."

The neuroscience of learning underscores their findings and provides a neurological explanation. Imagine the mental state of a young person who faces the very real possibility of being physically attacked on the way to or from school or being shaken down in the lavatory for lunch money or a new jacket. Predictably, that student would be less focused on learning about gerunds or cellular mitosis and more focused on avoiding the next confrontation. As noted in Chapter 1, the brain gives priority to potential threats to its survival or well-being. Whenever students fear for their physical safety, their limbic brains are on high alert, and *fight, flight, or freeze* responses are likely manifest. Especially for students who have stressful experiences beyond the classroom, it is necessary for them to feel protected and safe from violence and intimidation. Not surprisingly, in schools or classrooms that are not safe and orderly, deep learning of academic material is less likely.

Although a relatively small portion of the overall school population may be exposed to physical dangers, for many of today's youth, a less extreme but much more prominent threat hovers in the psychological realm. Whether in the form of teasing, being excluded from a lunch table group, or the modern-era torment of online bullying via social media, psychological stressors related to peer interactions (real or virtual) affect most students at some time during their school years.

A more mundane dimension of psychological safety in the classroom has to do with the extent to which students feel a sense of order and routine. When the parameters of acceptable behavior are unclear, classroom routines are lacking, materials are disorganized, or rules are inconsistently applied, students can become confused, distracted, and unruly. Accordingly, effective teachers are effective classroom managers and establish a clear set of rules, procedures, and routines at the start of the school year. When a class is well managed, it is safe, predictable, and focused on learning (Wong, Wong, Rogers, & Brooks, 2012).

The benefits of working to establish a safe and supportive school and classroom community cannot be overstated. Students in a supportive community do not fear that their instructor or classmates could harm their emotions, property, or bodies. Such a community is grounded in trust—between the educator and the students as well as among the students. Students who feel safe in their learning environment tend to be more self-confident, are willing and able to exchange ideas, participate even when mistakes are possible, and collaborate successfully.

Teachers' Acceptance

Researchers have shown that teachers' perceptions of their students' learning abilities can influence the achievement of those learners (Good, 1987). Factors found to potentially influence teacher expectations include student behavior in the classroom, race, social class, appearance, and information about past performance found in cumulative folders (Dusek & Joseph, 1983). Accordingly, students' sense of whether a teacher believes they are capable of successful learning may have an impact on their willingness to put forth effort on subject-matter learning. Research from the field of health care suggests a similar impact on the outcomes of medical interventions; when patients perceive that their doctors authentically care about them, they are more likely to comply with the regimens that physicians prescribe and realize the benefits (Banerjee & Sanyal, 2012; Cleary & McNeil, 1988).

Simple actions can communicate to students that you want to get to know them as individuals and believe that they are capable of learning. Actions such as greeting students in the morning or at the start of a class period, calling them by their first or preferred name, distributing earned praise equally, and avoiding "teacher's pets" help to create a supportive emotional climate in the classroom.

Many teachers recognize that taking a little time at the start of a new school term to get to know their students personally can pay valuable dividends throughout the year. The information you gather can help you see ways to connect content to kids. Perhaps more important, it signals to students that you care about them as individuals. Here are examples of practical methods for gathering information early in the school year to help you learn about your students' prior experiences, interests, and learning strengths and needs:

- Ask students to write a letter to you (and their other teachers) describing themselves as learners. Here are a few sample prompts:
  - *What subjects (or aspects of a particular subject) do you most enjoy? Why?*
  - *What subjects (or aspects of a particular subject) do you least enjoy? Why?*
  - *In what area of school do you excel?*
  - *What areas do you find most difficult?*
  - *How do you learn best?*

- *What do you want your teachers to know that will help them help you learn best?*

Note: Students incapable of extended writing may be allowed to use a recording device.

- Have students write a brief biography of their life to date. Ask them to relate their most vivid (positive) memory and include information relevant to their history as a student.
- Ask parents to write a letter to you describing their child. Here are some sample prompts:
  - *What are your child's interests and hobbies?*
  - *In what areas of school does your child excel? What areas does your child find most difficult?*
  - *How does your child learn best (e.g., listening, observing, doing)?*
  - *What do you want me to know that will help me help your child learn best?*
- Invite older students to create a "life map" timeline of key events in their past *and* a future map indicating where they plan or hope to be in 5 years and 10 years.
- Ask students to conduct a peer interview using questions such as those listed above. Then have each student introduce their partner to the class, using the information gathered through the interview.
- Ask students who know each other to complete a peer nomination form. Here are sample prompts:
  - *Who would you ask to help you if you get stuck on class work or homework?*
  - *With whom would you prefer to work in a group?*
  - *Who would you not wish to have in your group?*
  - *Who are the most serious students in this class?*
  - *Who are the most creative students in this class?*
  - *Who could best take charge of the class if the teacher had to leave the room?*
- Let students know that you respect them and are responsive to their feelings by inviting them to tell you what characteristics they find in their best teachers. Student lists are often quite similar in that most students seek the qualities in their teachers that they also seek in friends—for example, being fair, not showing favorites, being honest, being prepared, listening to their perspectives, and

having a good sense of humor. A class list of the most common characteristics can be generated and posted.

- To demonstrate that you value their opinions, let students know that about every six to eight weeks they will have an opportunity to give you a "report card" with grades on the items from the class list that was generated. (The report cards can be submitted anonymously to eliminate students' fears of being penalized for any negative ratings.) You can consider their "marks" and report back to them on areas you need to work on and how you hope to improve in those areas.

In general, we can say that a positive learning environment is enhanced when students feel known and accepted by teachers, administrators, coaches, and other adults in a school. Perhaps the importance of teacher acceptance is best captured by a learner's aphorism: "I don't care what you know until I know that you care!"

Peer Acceptance

Acceptance by the adults in a school is significant, but perhaps more important for some students, especially adolescents, is acceptance by their peers. Although a student's interactions with peers extend well beyond the walls of a school or an individual classroom, educators have taken steps to attend to the various social stressors that can interfere with optimal learning. For example, some secondary schools have established peer-mentoring programs to strengthen relationships among students and offer peer-based support for students in need (Ross, 2016). We have witnessed the spread of antibullying programs in response to the physical and psychological aggressions that some students experience. And as previously noted, some schools have instituted social-emotional learning programs that teach a set of social skills, including effective communication, decision making, impulse control, conflict resolution, anger management, and empathy.

In addition to district- or school-level initiatives and programs, there are specific actions that teachers can take to help establish an accepting and collaborative learning environment in their classrooms. Consider these:

- Begin the school year with get-to-know-you activities. Here are some examples:

- Have students interview each other and introduce their partner to the class. It's beneficial to pair students who do not already know each other well and remind students that they need to share positive attributes in their peer introductions.
- Conduct a scavenger hunt to *find someone in the class who* ____ (e.g., has a pet, has traveled to another state or country, plays an instrument, enjoys sports, shares your favorite game).
- Have students complete "all about me" index cards in response to prompts, such as *My favorite subject is* ____*; My favorite hobby is* ____*; When I grow up, I want to be* ____*; I am most happy when* ____. Then, have students share their cards and eventually post them on a bulletin board.

• Create a bulletin board that showcases the interests and talents of class members.

• Prepare a list of "class experts" based on areas of high interest and expertise that classmates might value, such as subject-area knowledge, skills in art, skateboarding, computer gaming, or dancing. A list of students' names and specialties can then be shared.

• Have students help generate class rules, with an emphasis on respecting the well-being and learning of others. Post the list and use it as a behavioral reference.

• Develop a list of specific behaviors associated with an accepting and supportive classroom environment, such as respect for others, empathy, avoiding put-downs, no bullying, and supporting each other's learning. Then, have students help generate a list of observable indicators for each of the behaviors. Post the completed lists and highlight those behaviors when you see them. Have students periodically self-assess themselves on these behaviors.

• Speak with students who violate the peer-acceptance norms. Offer specific feedback on what they have done that is insensitive or hurtful to others, and help them adjust future behavior.

• Conduct regular class meetings to build trust, enhance communication and problem-solving skills, and encourage positive relationships. Teach and employ simple strategies during the meetings—for example, sit in a circle; pass a talking stick when someone has something to say; have students acknowledge one quality they appreciate in a classmate before expressing a concern.

- Hold a weekly "sharing" session in which students write about two positive events that occurred in their lives and one not-so-positive event (along with what they could have done to make it better or what they learned from it).
- Regularly post student work that (1) shows quality and (2) reflects progress or improvement. Celebrate both achievement *and* growth!
- Regularly use cooperative learning strategies to involve students in interactive learning. Directly teach and model effective group behaviors. Vary group size and composition so that students have opportunities to work with a variety of their peers on varied tasks. Also rotate the group roles (e.g., facilitator, time keeper, summarizer, process observer) so that students develop effective collaborative skills. Have students regularly self-assess both individual and group effectiveness.

Here's a historical note: Recognition of the significance of student and staff relationships gave impetus to a large-scale educational initiative supported by the Bill and Melinda Gates Foundation. The initiative involved reorganizing large, comprehensive high schools into "small schools" to make it more likely that every student would be known and have an adult advocate in the building (Strauss, 2014a). Although the mission to create a more personalized school climate was well intended, subsequent evaluations of these small-school projects failed to show any substantive improvements in student achievement as was expected. Our analysis of the initiative was that it was incomplete; that is, while attending to the important dimensions of climate and connectedness, the initiative did not *simultaneously* address the necessary curriculum, instruction, and assessment reforms needed to engage learners in deep and relevant learning.

To be blunt, having smaller schools alone will not lead to deeper learning and enhanced performance if the instructional focus remains on superficial coverage of content material and multiple-choice testing of factual knowledge predominates. With this point in mind, let's now examine other factors that the brain needs for optimal learning.

Task Variables

The second broad category in Figure 7.1 references three variables associated with the learning and assessment tasks that students encounter in school: task *clarity*, task *relevance*, and learners' *perceived capacity to be successful*. We'll now explore how each of these affects students' motivation, attention, effort, and willingness to persevere with challenging tasks.

Clarity

As noted in Chapter 3, the human brain is a goal-directed organ, and the implications for school learning are straightforward: learners are more likely to focus their efforts when there is a clear and worthwhile learning goal. Conversely, when the goal is unclear or irrelevant to students, it is unlikely that they will maintain attention or try their best. Clarity in the classroom starts with the teacher. Researcher John Hattie (2008, 2013) has conducted meta-analyses on studies of instructional practices and found that teacher clarity is one of the most salient factors for positive effects on student achievement. When teachers use the backward design process of UbD to plan, they should be crystal clear about the intended learning outcomes of units and associated lessons (Stage 1), as well as the methods by which student learning will be assessed (Stage 2). They can then communicate the goals and assessments to help students know (1) what they are to be learning, (2) why this learning is important (in school and beyond), and (3) how their learning will be assessed (Wiggins & McTighe, 2004, 2012). Here are practical and efficient techniques for how to do this:

- Directly state the learning goals at the beginning of the unit, in conjunction with the overall year or course goals.
- Present the rationale for the unit or course goals.
- Invite students to generate questions about the unit topic—the *W* in KWL.
- Ask students to identify personal learning goals related to the unit topic.
- Post and discuss essential question(s) at the start of the unit.
- Present the culminating assessments and performance task requirements.
- Involve students in identifying appropriate evaluation criteria for the upcoming work.

- Review scoring rubrics for performance tasks or projects.
- Show models/exemplars of expected products or performances to make the success criteria found in rubrics tangible to students.

Assessment expert Richard Stiggins (1996) offers an aphorism that reminds us of the importance of clarity to learning: "Students can hit any target that they can see and that holds still for them."

Relevance

An important psychological factor that affects learning has to do with the extent to which students see value and utility in what they are being asked to learn. Students' interest and motivation suffer if they do not see purpose, as evidenced by questions they often ask, such as "Why do we need to know this?" or "When will I ever be able to use this?" Responses such as "Trust me, you'll thank me later" or "Because it may be on the state test" are not the most compelling reasons to convince learners to put forth maximum effort on their schoolwork. Think about it: how many adults would sit still for prolonged instruction on material for which they saw no usefulness over the short—or long—term?

Here is how educational author and consultant Willard Daggett (2009) describes the nature of relevance:

> Relevance refers to learning in which students apply core knowledge, concepts, or skills, to solve real-world problems. Relevant learning is interdisciplinary and contextual. It is created, for example, through authentic problems or tasks, simulations, service learning, connecting concepts to current issues and teaching others.

Daggett contends that there can be no rigor without relevance.

Teachers who use UbD when designing lessons and assessments are prompted to frame learning around big ideas, essential questions, and authentic performance tasks—and each of these elements can convey value and relevance to learners. Authentic tasks have a side benefit: like a game in athletics or a play in theater, they highlight the "end" toward which we must prepare. Thus they provide the rationale and motivation for learning the basics that will be needed for successful performance. Consider how many athletes would endure painful conditioning workouts or repeatedly practice sports skills if they were *not* striving to improve their performance in forthcoming games or meets. In other words, learning the rules of the game and mastering the skills are means to a worthwhile goal (playing the game), just as mastering grade-level standards are the building blocks that enable authentic and valued performances.

Here are specific ways to help learners see relevance in schoolwork:

- Identify people and places beyond the classroom where the targeted knowledge and skills are applied.
- Frame learning around big ideas and essential questions that give meaning to the content being explored.
- Invite students to link their own interests and long-term goals (if they have them) to specific content being learned.
- Frame learning around relevant and authentic tasks (using GRASPS, as described in Chapter 4) that specify a role, a target audience, an authentic product or performance, and genuine constraints.
- Tell students about the culminating performance tasks at the start of a new unit so that they will have the "end in mind" as they are learning the basics. Show how mastering specific skills will support their performance.
- Present and discuss success criteria in advance so that students will know what the qualities of effective performance are. (As an alternative, guide students in generating the success criteria to build understanding and ownership.)

Perceived Capacity to Succeed

The neuroscience of learning underscores the need for students to believe that they have the capacity to succeed at learning new things and perform well on associated tasks. Like the fox who is unable to catch healthy adult rabbits and eventually stops chasing them, students who experience the pattern of multiple failures in school may conclude that they will never be good at math, art, or learning a language, and they will therefore be less inclined to try. Such a pattern could easily lead to a fixed mindset, in which effort and achievement are decoupled in the learner's mind.

The good news is that teachers can play a pivotal role in influencing students' perceptions of their ability to learn. As noted throughout this book, learners need achievable challenges—worthy learning goals that are within their grasp. Thus teachers should not only plan their curriculum backward from worthy goals but also support students on their varied learning trajectories toward those ends. There are three primary ways in which teachers can encourage and bolster learners—by design:

- *Offer personalized support* by using the ideas for differentiation listed in Chapter 6. When students see that a teacher believes in their ability to succeed and is actively supporting *their* learning, they will be more likely to put forth effort and persevere to master academics.
- *Provide specific, ongoing feedback.* Just as athletic coaches use practice sessions to provide guided practice and feedback to help players strengthen their skills needed for the game, teachers enable students' successes through the use of nongraded, formative assessments with feedback. When feedback is a regular and expected component of classroom instruction, learners are empowered to achieve.
- *Look for opportunities to highlight students' improvements* and celebrate their incremental progress toward learning goals. As the video game model demonstrates, learners are more apt to persist in an activity as long as they can see that they are making headway. Teachers can encourage this effect by breaking complex tasks into smaller, attainable chunks; by providing scaffolds (cues, strategies, and tips); by allowing self-pacing with appropriate choice; and by highlighting the results achieved because of students' efforts.

A learner's awareness of progress toward goals facilitates information travel through the amygdala. As students have repeated experiences in recognizing that their focused efforts can result in progress and learning achievements, you'll see them tackle—and persevere through—more challenging learning tasks, seek and accept corrective feedback, and be willing to make needed revisions or practice more diligently. Establishing these patterns in your classroom reinforces a growth mindset, which is crucial for students' success in school and in life.

Teaching Students About Their "Brain Owner" Powers

We conclude this book with the recommendation that school curricula build in structured opportunities for students to learn how their brains work and how to self-manage various cognitive and emotional states (Willis, 2009a, 2009b, 2009c). Such attention to the "brain owner's manual" helps students recognize various stressors or perceived threats that can trigger their brains into the modes of *fight, flight, or freeze*. It will help them to understand dysfunctional behavior (e.g., acting out, distracting others, avoiding teachers' questions, hiding in the bathroom, or skipping class) as manifestations of the brain's natural stress responses and to develop positive alternatives for managing that stress. They will learn about *fixed* versus *growth* mindsets and develop practical and personalized strategies for mastering new material and dealing with learning challenges. Further, they will comprehend how, through their own brain's neuroplasticity, they can grow their intelligence and succeed as learners. When you teach students about the workings and power of their brains, they'll hold the keys for successful operation of the most powerful tool they'll ever own.

Glossary

achievable challenge A level of difficulty for goals that is challenging for the individual yet still attainable. *See also* **zone of proximal development**.

achievement target A desired result or learning goal. *See also* **desired result, outcome**.

affective filter A neurochemical reaction to an emotional state of stress during which a person is not responsive to processing, learning, and storing new information. This affective filter is represented by objective physical evidence on neuroimaging of the amygdala, which becomes metabolically hyperactive during periods of high stress. This hyper-stimulated state prevents new information from passing through the amygdala to reach the information-processing centers of the brain. *See also* **amygdala**.

AMT An acronym referring to three different types of educational goals: *A* = *Acquisition*, referring to knowledge and skills that students should acquire; *M* = *Meaning Making*, referring to the meanings (or understandings) that we want students to come to; *T* = *Transfer*, referring to how students should be able to apply their learning to new situations. These different goal types are significant because each requires somewhat different approaches to instruction and assessment.

amygdala Part of the limbic system in the temporal lobe of the brain. It was first believed to function as a brain center for responding only to anxiety and fear. However, it is now believed to be related to many kinds of intense emotions. It appears to play a major role in emotional processing and impulsivity in adolescents. When the amygdala senses threat (which for students can mean feelings of stress, anxiety, frustration, or helplessness), it becomes overactivated (displaying high metabolic activity). When the amygdala is in this state of overactivation, new information coming through the sensory intake areas of the brain cannot pass through the amygdala's affective filter to gain access to the memory circuits, thus diminishing learning. *See also* **affective filter, limbic system**.

analytic rubric, analytic scoring A type of rubric or scoring that identifies several distinct traits to use in evaluating student products and performances, with each evaluated independently. For example, in the analytic scoring of written essays, we might evaluate five traits: organization, use of detail, attention to audience, persuasiveness, and conventions. Analytic scoring is in contrast with holistic scoring, whereby a judge forms a single overall impression about a performance. *See also* **holistic rubric, holistic scoring**.

anchor Sample of work or performance used to illustrate the specific performance standard for each level of a rubric. For example, attached to a four-level rubric in writing would be two or three samples of writing that illustrate the qualities of a four-, three-, two-, and one-level performance. An anchor for the top score level is often called the "exemplar."

application One of the six facets of understanding. The ability to apply knowledge and skill in diverse situations provides evidence of understanding. *See also* **facets of understanding**.

assessment Any systematic basis for making inferences about student learning, usually based on various sources of evidence. Educational assessment can employ a variety of techniques (e.g., a test, a quiz, a performance task or project, an observation, an interview) for different purposes (e.g., formative and summative). Effective assessment requires a balance of techniques because each technique is limited and prone to error.

Assessment is sometimes viewed as synonymous with evaluation, though common usage differs. We can assess a student's strengths and weaknesses without placing a value, judgment, or a grade on that performance. *See also* **evaluation, formative assessment, summative assessment**.

authentic task, authentic assessment A task or assessment that simulates or replicates important, real-world challenges containing genuine goals or purposes, audiences, and constraints.

axon The connection that extends from a neuron and carries the electrically coded message to the dendrites of other neurons. *See also* **dendrite, neuron**.

backward design An approach to designing a curriculum or a unit that begins with the end in mind and plans toward that end. Backward design may be thought of as purposeful task analysis: given a goal to be accomplished, how do we get there? When applied to curriculum design, UbD proposes a three-stage backward design process: Stage 1—Identify desired results (learning goals or outcomes); Stage 2—Determine assessment evidence (of achieving those goals); Stage 3—Develop the learning plan and lessons to help students achieve the desired results.

big idea In Understanding by Design, a transferable idea—concept, principle, theme, process—that should serve as the focal point of curricula, instruction, and assessment. *See also* **understanding**.

Bloom's taxonomy The common name of a schema, developed by Benjamin Bloom and his colleagues, for six cognitive levels: Knowledge, Comprehension, Application, Analysis, Synthesis, and Evaluation, with the last three commonly referred to as "higher order."

buy-in Motivation and willingness to put forth effort toward achieving a goal. Positive climate and prevention of high stressors promote information passage through the amygdala to the prefrontal cortex. Motivation and effort increase when the brain expects pleasure. Factors related to buy-in include personal relevance, prediction, and learning activities connecting to students' interests and strengths. *See also* **amygdala**.

cerebral cortex In the brain, the outermost layer of the cerebrum, which contains neurons. *See also* **neuron**.

cognition Thinking and all of the mental processes related to thinking.

concept A mental construct or category represented by a word. Concepts include both tangible objects (e.g., chair, rabbit) and abstract ideas (e.g., democracy, bravery).

content standard *See* **standard**.

control group In an experiment, this subset of members does not receive manipulation or treatment, but may receive a placebo.

correlation A connection or relationship between two or more things or sets of scientific data. Correlation between two things or situations is *not* the same as causation, in which one is proven to directly cause the other.

course A set of curricular units making up a semester-long or year-long course of study. The term is widely used at the secondary and collegiate levels.

coverage An approach to instruction that superficially teaches and tests content knowledge, irrespective of student understanding or engagement. The term generally has a negative connotation: it implies that the goal is to march through a body of material (often a textbook) within a specified time frame.

criteria Guidelines, rules, or principles by which student responses, products, or performances are judged. To ask, "What are the criteria?" amounts to asking, "How will we evaluate student work? What should we look for when examining students' products or performances to know if they are successful?" Wiggins and McTighe (2012) suggest four broad categories of criteria: *content*, *process*, *quality*, and *impact*.

critical period A window of opportunity when a specialized type of learning can occur. Although learning can take place at any time, it will be easier during this period.

curriculum From its Latin root, literally "the course to be run." In Understanding by Design, the term refers to the explicit and comprehensive plan developed and implemented toward a set of long-term goals or outcomes (e.g., standards, 21st century skills, dispositions).

deductive reasoning The ability to use stored, existing prior knowledge to predict new rules and appropriate responses to new information or situations perceived as being similar to these past experiences.

dendrite A branched extension that sprouts from the arms (axons) or the cell bodies of neurons. Dendrites conduct electrical impulses toward the neighboring neurons, thus connecting neurons into circuits of related information. A single nerve may possess many dendrites.

Because new dendrites grow as branches from frequently activated neurons, the size and number of dendrites increase in response to learned skills, experience, and information storage. *See also* **axon, neuron**.

design To plan the form and structure of something or the pattern or motif of a work of art. In education, teachers are designers in both senses, aiming to develop purposeful, coherent, effective, and engaging lessons, units, and courses of study and accompanying assessments to achieve identified results. At the heart of Understanding by Design is the idea that what happens *before* the teacher gets in the classroom may be as or more important than the teaching that goes on inside the classroom.

design standards The specific standards used to evaluate the quality of curricular designs. The design standards for Understanding by Design have two purposes: (1) to guide self-assessment and peer reviews to identify design strengths and needed improvements; and (2) to provide a mechanism for quality control, a means of validating curricular designs.

desired result A term used in Stage 1 of backward design to refer to any learning goal or outcome. Desired results can include various goal types—knowledge, skills, understandings, transfer goals, and dispositions (habits of mind).

discrepant event Something that does not appear or turn out the way the brain expects. The sense of disequilibrium experienced with a discrepant event motivates students' attention and curiosity as the brain seeks an explanation for its incorrect prediction.

dopamine A neurotransmitter most associated with attention, decision making, executive function, and reward-stimulated learning. As shown through neuroimaging, the release of dopamine in the brain has been found to increase in response to rewards and positive experiences. Scans reveal greater dopamine release while subjects are playing, laughing, exercising, and receiving acknowledgment (e.g., praise) for achievement.

dopamine-reward response Elevated dopamine release and circulation in the brain that manifests as an increase in pleasure, curiosity, attention, and motivation to pursue goals that are the source of the motivating arousal.

electroencephalography (EEG) A type of imaging method that records the electrical activity of the brain. It produces a dynamic image of the brain—an image of the brain working.

empathy One of the six facets of understanding. Empathy, the ability to "walk in another's shoes," to escape one's own emotional reactions to grasp another's, is central to the most common colloquial use of the term *understanding*. *See also* **facets of understanding**.

encoding The process by which the brain receives information and converts it into memory.

enduring understanding In Understanding by Design, an important, transferrable idea that has lasting value beyond the classroom. An enduring understanding specifies what we want students to come to understand about a topic or process.

essential question An open-ended question meant to engage student thinking and promote inquiry. Unlike leading or guiding questions that have a "correct" answer, essential questions are debatable and meant to recur; teachers revisit them over time to help learners develop and deepen their understanding of important "big" ideas.

evaluation A process for judging the quality, proficiency, or depth of learning.

executive functions Mental skills that are enabled by the neural networks for processing of information in the prefrontal cortex (and associated connections) and that allow conscious control over emotions and thoughts. Examples include organizing, analyzing, sorting, connecting, planning, prioritizing, sequencing, self-monitoring, self-correcting, assessing, abstracting, problem solving, attention focusing, and linking information to appropriate actions. *See also* **prefrontal cortex**.

experiment A scientific endeavor in which a researcher manipulates one or more variables to determine what effect the manipulation has on another variable.

experimental group In an experiment, this subset of members receives some sort of treatment or manipulation.

explanation One of the six facets of understanding. Understanding involves more than just knowing information. We expect a person with understanding to be able to "show your work," to explain and justify *why*, not just state the facts. *See also* **facets of understanding**.

extrinsic motivation A desire to perform a behavior because of rewards that come from the external world. *See also* **intrinsic motivation**.

facets of understanding A way in which a person's understanding manifests itself. Understanding by Design identifies six kinds of understanding: application, empathy, explanation, interpretation, perspective, and self-knowledge. The facets are used as a way to gather assessment evidence of understanding. Note that all six facets are not necessary to show evidence of understanding. For example, a student could demonstrate understanding of a mathematical concept through application and explanation, whereas perspective and empathy would not apply. *See also* **application, empathy, explanation, interpretation, perspective, self-knowledge**.

fixed mindset A state of mind in which an individual believes that ability to learn and succeed is predetermined by innate ability or fixed intelligence, and that effort will not make a difference. This attitude contrasts with a growth mindset, in which a person believes that intelligence is modifiable, and that effort and persistence can improve performance. *See also* **neuroplasticity, growth mindset**.

flow A mental state characterized by full immersion in what an individual is doing at a particular time. The individual experiences positive affect and intrinsic reward while in the flow state.

focused attention Intentional or effortful directing of one's attention to sensory input, information, or an experience.

formative assessment Ongoing assessments are used to monitor student learning and provide feedback to both teachers and students to make adjustments that improve learning and performance. The purpose of formative assessment is to inform, not evaluate; thus, formative assessment results should not be graded. *See also* **summative assessment**.

frontal lobe The part of the brain that is the most anterior lobe of the cerebrum; it contains the motor cortex and other centers of executive function that organize and arrange information and coordinates the production of language and the focusing of attention. *See also* **executive function**.

functional magnetic resonance imaging (fMRI) A type of imaging that produces dynamic images of the brain. Measuring changes in oxygenated blood flow to areas of the brain enables interpretations based on the knowledge that more active regions of the brain receive more oxygen. Most fMRI scans are conducted while subjects are exposed to visual, auditory, or tactile stimuli, revealing the brain structures that are activated by these experiences.

glial cell A nonneuronal cell in the nervous system. Such cells nourish, support, and complement the activity of neurons in the brain. *See also* **neuron**.

goal-directed behavior Action directed toward achieving a specific purpose. It includes the ability to monitor one's progress toward the goal and make adjustments as needed in response to setbacks or new information.

gray matter A term referring to the brownish-gray color of the nerve-cell bodies and dendrites of the brain and spinal cord as compared with white matter, which is primarily composed of supportive tissue. Neurons, which are darker than other brain matter, are most dense in the cortex, the outer layer of the brain. *See also* **dendrite, neuron**.

growth mindset A state of mind in which an individual recognizes that achievement is the result of effort and persistence, not just innate ability, resulting in a feeling of confidence in ability to learn and to change one's brain. *See also* **fixed mindset, neuroplasticity**.

hippocampus The center in the brain where sensory intake links with related information activated from long-term memory to encode new short-term memory. The hippocampus binds the separate aspects of the experience into storable patterns of relational memories.

holistic rubric, holistic scoring A scoring tool or method of scoring yielding a single score based upon an overall impression of a student's product or performance. Holistic scoring is distinguished from analytic scoring, in which distinct traits of performance are evaluated independently. *See also* **analytic rubric, analytic scoring**.

inductive reasoning The process of recognizing or constructing more generalized concepts, principles, or rules based on specific information and examples. Examples include evaluating the rules that appear to apply to situations and using those consistencies to make accurate predictions or interpretations of new, related information.

interpretation One of the six facets of understanding. To interpret is to make sense of and find meaning in human experience, data, and texts. *See also* **facets of understanding**.

intrinsic motivation A desire that comes from within, that seeks to perform a certain behavior for its own sake. *See also* **extrinsic motivation**.

KWL A graphic organizer with columns to be filled in throughout a unit. The letters stand for *what I know, what I want to know,* and *what I learned.*

limbic system A group of interconnected structures deep in the brain, including the amygdala, the hippocampus, and portions of the frontal and temporal lobes, involved in emotion, motivation, behavior, and reactions. *See also* **amygdala, hippocampus, frontal lobe, temporal lobe**.

longitudinal rubric A scoring tool that assesses performance according to a novice-expert continuum, independent of age or grade level, to track progress (or lack thereof) toward a standard. For example, the American Council on the Teaching of Foreign Languages (ACTFL) uses a longitudinal rubric for charting the progress of all language development over time. Also called a *developmental rubric.*

long-term memory A type of memory that is durable and retrievable. It is formed as a result of the brain's neuroplasticity, whereby activation of the neural network transforms short-term memory into long-term memory through actions such as repetition and recognition of relationships. These actions result in physical changes in the brain (the production of more synapses with strong and stronger connections between neurons) to create long-term memory. *See also* **neuron, neuroplasticity, short-term memory, synapse**.

metacognition An executive function whereby individuals monitor their cognition and control their mental processes.

mode, performance mode The type or method of performance being demonstrated and assessed. Modes of performance include written, oral, visual, and kinesthetic.

motor cortex An area in the frontal lobe of the brain that directs fine motor coordination. *See also* **frontal lobe**.

myelin Fat-protein layers that form sheaths around most axons to insulate them and protect the nerve fiber. Myelin increases speed of conduction of nerve impulses through the axon, resulting in more efficient information access and retrieval. *See also* **axon, myelination**.

myelination The formation of a myelin sheath around a nerve fiber, which insulates it and makes it more efficient. *See also* **myelin**.

nervous system One of the body's major systems, consisting of the brain, the spinal cord, and the extensive pathways of nervous tissue located throughout the body that permit communication between specialized cells called neurons. *See also* **neuron**.

neural network A system of neurons communicating with each other in circuits by sending coded electrochemical messages through connections involving axons, synapses, and dendrites. *See also* **axon, dendrite, neuron, synapse**.

neuroimaging (functional brain imaging) The use of techniques to directly or indirectly demonstrate the structure, function, or biochemical status of the brain. *Structural* neuroimaging reveals the overall structure of the brain; *functional* neuroimaging provides visualization of the processing of sensory information coming to the brain and of commands going from the brain to the body. This processing is visualized directly as areas of the brain "light up" as a result of increased metabolism, blood flow, oxygen use, or glucose uptake. Functional brain imaging reveals neural activity in particular brain regions as the brain performs discrete cognitive tasks.

neuron A kind of specialized cell in the brain and throughout the nervous system that conducts electrical impulses to, from, and within the brain. Neurons are composed of a main cell body, a single axon for outgoing electrical signals, and a varying number of dendrites for incoming signals in electrical form. An average adult brain has more than 80 billion neurons. Neurons differ from other cells because of their unique ability to communicate rapidly with one another over great distances and with great precision. *See also* **axon, dendrite**.

neuronal circuit A system of electrochemical connections by which neurons communicate with each other by sending coded messages.

When there is repeated stimulation of specific patterns between the same group of neurons, their connecting circuit becomes more developed and more accessible to efficient stimulation and response. This process explains how practice results in more successful recall. *See also* **neuron**.

neuroplasticity The ability of the brain's synapses, neurons, dendrites, and myelin-coated axons to change their properties in response to usage (stimulation).When there is repeated stimulation of a circuit of linked neurons, the connections become more developed, resulting in more efficient retrieval of the information they hold. *See also* **axon, dendrite, myelin, neuron, synapse**.

neurotransmitters Brain proteins that are released by the electrical impulses on one side of the synapse (axonal terminal) and then float across the synaptic gap carrying the information with them to stimulate the nerve ending (dendrite) of the next cell in the pathway. Once the neurotransmitter is taken up by the dendrite nerve ending, the electric impulse is reactivated in that dendrite to travel along to the next nerve. Neurotransmitters in the brain include serotonin, tryptophan, acetylcholine, dopamine, and others that transport information across synapses and also circulate through the brain, much like hormones, to influence larger regions of the brain. When neurotransmitters are depleted, by too much information traveling through a nerve circuit without a break, the speed of transmission along the nerve slows down to a less efficient level. *See also* **axon, dendrite, dopamine, neuroimaging, serotonin, synapse**.

nucleus accumbens (NAc) A small structure deep in the limbic system on each side of the brain that holds a large quantity of dopamine, which it sends through channels into upper regions of the brain. The primary receiving area for this dopamine is in the prefrontal cortex, receiving it from activations of the dopamine-reward response. *See also* **dopamine, limbic system, prefrontal cortex**.

occipital lobe The part of the brain that primarily processes visual information.

open-ended task or question A term used to describe a task or question if it does not lead to a single "correct" answer. This does not imply that all answers are of equal value, however. When addressing open-ended tasks and questions, students should be expected to explain, justify, support, and defend their responses.

outcome In education, a learning goal or desired result.

patterning The process whereby the brain perceives sensory data and generates patterns by relating new information to previously learned material. Education is about increasing the patterns that students can use, recognize, and communicate. Whenever new material is presented in such a way that students see relationships, they can generate greater brain cell activity (formation of new neural connections) and achieve more successful patterns for storage and retrieval of long-term memory.

performance task A learning activity or an assessment that directs students to apply their learning and develop a product or performance. Because performance tasks generally do not have a single "correct" answer or solution method, evaluations of student products or performances are based on judgments guided by criteria.

perspective One of the six facets of understanding. Perspective involves the ability to recognize other plausible points of view. *See also* **facets of understanding**.

placebo Anything that is given as a real treatment, but in fact is not.

portfolio A representative collection of one's work. In academic subject areas, a portfolio often serves two distinct purposes: (1) providing documentation of a student's work over time, and (2) serving as the basis for evaluation of that work.

positron emission tomography (PET scan) A neuroimaging technique that produces a three-dimensional image of functional processes in the body based on the detection of radiation from the emission of tiny particles attached to molecules of glucose and injected into the blood. PET scans measure the metabolism of glucose in the brain in response to certain activities. The rate at which specific regions of the brain use the glucose is recorded while the subject is engaged in various cognitive activities. These recordings can be used to produce maps of areas of high brain activity associated with particular cognitive functions.

prefrontal cortex The most anterior region of the frontal lobe of the brain. The prefrontal cortex is the neural network hub that controls executive decision-making functions with intake and output to almost all other regions of the brain. In addition, the prefrontal cortex is part of the system by which long-term memories are constructed and emotions can be consciously evaluated.

prerequisite knowledge and skill The knowledge and skill required to successfully achieve a new learning goal or perform a task.

prior knowledge Information that students have already acquired through formal teaching or personal experience, stored in their long-term memory banks.

pruning The destruction of neurons when they are not used. A baby's brain overproduces brain cells (neurons) and connections between brain cells (synapses) and then starts pruning them back around the age of 3. The second wave of synapse formation occurs just before puberty and is followed by another phase of pruning. Pruning allows the brain to consolidate learning by removing unused neurons and synapses and wrapping white matter (myelin) around the neuronal networks that are more frequently used, to stabilize and strengthen them. *See also* **myelin, neuron, synapse**.

receptor site Location on the dendrite of a postsynaptic neuron that is specialized to bind only with a particular neurotransmitter molecule. *See also* **dendrite, neuron, neurotransmitter**.

reliable, reliability In measurement, a term that refers to the accuracy of a score. In performance assessment, reliability is considered in two ways: (1) To what extent can we generalize from the single (or sample of) performance to the student's performance in general? Is the score truly representative of the student's general capacities and patterns of results? (2) What is the likelihood that different judges will evaluate the same performance in the same way? The second question involves what is typically termed *inter-rater reliability*.

reticular activating system (RAS) A group of neurons located in the brain stem that alerts the forebrain to important stimuli. This lower part of the posterior brain filters all incoming stimuli and makes the "decision" as to what sensory input is attended to or ignored. The main categories that focus the attention of the RAS include novelty (changes in the environment), surprise, danger, and movement. *See also* **neuron**.

rubric A criterion-based scoring tool for evaluating student products or performances. A rubric consists of a set of evaluative criteria and a performance scale (e.g., four points) for distinguishing degrees of understanding, skill proficiency, or product/performance quality. Two general types of rubrics—analytic and holistic—are widely used to judge student products and performances. Holistic rubrics provide an overall impression of a student's work. Holistic rubrics yield a single score or rating for a product or performance. An analytic rubric divides a product or performance into distinct traits or dimensions and judges each independently. *See also* **analytic rubric, analytic scoring; holistic rubric, holistic scoring; scoring scale**.

scaffolding A term referring to the provision of different levels of support during instruction to accommodate the individual needs of students. Rather than simplifying the task, the instructor simplifies the role of the learner by providing different levels of prompts or hints.

scientific method A procedure for conducting and carrying out research. The scientific method includes making observations, asking questions, forming a hypothesis, creating an experiment, recording and analyzing results, and drawing conclusions.

scoring scale An equally divided continuum (number line) for use in evaluating performance. The scale identifies how many different scores, from high to low, will be used to differentiate degrees of understanding, skill proficiency, or product/performance quality.

self-knowledge One of the six facets of understanding. Self-knowledge refers to metacognition—thinking about one's thinking. Self-knowledge also involves the degree of awareness of one's biases and how these influence one's thinking, perceptions, and beliefs. *See also* **facets of understanding, metacognition**.

serotonin A neurotransmitter in the brain involved in learning, memory, mood regulation, attention, sleep, and arousal level. *See also* **neurotransmitter**.

short-term memory A type of memory that contains a small amount of information, held for a short period of time. Transforming short-term memory to long-term memory requires mental manipulation such as rehearsal or doing something with the new memory.

standard In education, a term with various meanings. Understanding by Design distinguishes among three types of standards: (1) content standards (what students should know and be able to do), (2) performance standards (how well students must do something); and (3) design standards (criteria by which curriculum and unit designs are judged).

standardized A term referring to a test or assessment in which the administrative conditions and protocol are uniform for all students.

summative assessment The purpose of summative assessment is to evaluate the degree to which students have achieved the targeted learning goals. Summative assessment results often serve as the basis for grades. *See also* **formative assessment**.

synapse (synaptic gap) A space, filled with spinal fluid, between the axon of one neuron and the dendrite of another, across which chemical neurotransmitters such as dopamine carry information. Before and after crossing the synapse as a chemical message, information is carried in an electrical state when it travels down the nerve. Once the neurotransmitter crosses the synaptic gap to the next nerve ending, it is converted back to an electric impulse. *See also* **axon, dendrite, neuron, neurotransmitter**.

template A guide or framework for designers. In UbD, the Unit Planning Template is a graphic organizer and conceptual guide that reflects and supports backward design. Each section of the UbD Template contains key questions, prompting the user to consider particular elements of curriculum design.

temporal lobe The outermost lobe on each side of the brain; it processes and stores information related to sound, as well as being part of the emotional limbic and memory storage systems.

top-down processing A term referring to the brain's processing of information that is knowledge based. It encompasses the ability to direct attention to a particular stimulus or event in the environment.

transfer A term that refers to the ability to apply learning effectively to a new situation.

understanding An insight into ideas, people, situations, and processes manifested in various appropriate performances. To understand is to make sense of what one knows, to be able to know why it's so, and to be able to use it in various situations and contexts.

unit Short for "unit of study." Although there are no definitive criteria for what a unit is, in general we describe a curriculum unit as a body of subject matter that focuses on a major topic (e.g., the Revolutionary War in America) or process (e.g., the research process) and that lasts between a few days and a few weeks—falling somewhere in length between a lesson and an entire course of study.

validity A term that refers to the inferences one can confidently draw about student learning based on the results of an assessment. Does the assessment or test measure what it purports to measure? Do the test results correlate with other performance results? Does the sample of questions or tasks accurately correlate with what students would do if we tested them on everything that was taught? Do the results have predictive value—do they correlate with likely future success in the subject in question? Some or all of these questions must have a "yes" answer for a test to be valid.

To be more precise, it is not an assessment or test itself that is valid; rather, validity refers to the extent to which its results permit valid inferences to be made.

WHERETO An acronym used to remind teachers to consider various aspects of a learning plan. *W*: **Where** are we going? Why? What is expected? *H*: How will we **hook** the students? *E1*: How will we **equip** students for expected performance? *R*: How will we help learners **rethink** or **revise**? *E2*: How will students self-**evaluate** and reflect on their learning? *T*: How will we **tailor** learning to varied needs, interests, and learning preferences? *O*: How will we **organize** and sequence the learning plan?

white matter A layer located just under the brain's outer layer of gray matter, comprising most of the deep parts of the brain. White matter is composed of connections between neurons, including dendrites, myelinated axons, and support cells called glia. *See also* **axon, dendrite, glial cell, gray matter, neuron**.

zone of actual development A term referring to a child's developmental level (or mental age) based on activities that the child can perform without assistance.

zone of proximal development A term referring to the difference between a child's actual developmental level and the child's potential to develop. This zone represents abilities in the child that are in the process of maturing. *See also* **achievable challenge**.

References

Absolum, M. (2006). *Clarity in the classroom: Assessment for learning*. Auckland, NZ: Hodder Education.

Anderson, R. C., Spiro, R. J., & Anderson, M. C. (1978). Schemata as scaffolding for the representation of information in connected discourse. *American Educational Research Journal, 15*(3), 433–440.

Armenta, C., Fritz, M., & Lyubomirsky, S. (2017). Functions of positive emotions: Gratitude as a motivator of self-improvement and positive change. *Emotion Review, 9*(3), 1–8.

Banerjee, A., & Sanyal, D. (2012). Dynamics of doctor-patient relationship: A cross-sectional study on concordance, trust, and patient enablement. *Journal of Family Community Medicine, 19*(1), 12–19.

Berridge, K. C., & Kringelbach, M. L. (2013). Neuroscience of affect: Brain mechanisms of pleasure and displeasure. *Current Opinion in Neurobiology, 23*(3), 294–303.

Beyer, B. (1997). *Improving student thinking: A comprehensive approach*. Boston: Allyn and Bacon.

Black, P., & Wiliam, D. (1998). Inside the black box: Raising standards through classroom assessment. *Phi Delta Kappan, 80*(2), 1–13.

Bloom, B. (Ed.). (1956). *Taxonomy of educational objectives, handbook 1: Cognitive domain*. Chicago: University of Chicago Press.

Bransford, J., Brown, A., & Cocking, R. (Ed.). (2000). *How people learn: Brain, mind, experience, and school: Expanded edition*. Washington, DC: National Academy Press.

Brookhart, S., & McTighe, J. (2017). *The formative assessment learning cycle*. (Quick Reference Guide). Alexandria, VA: ASCD.

Brown, A. (1985). Mental orthopedics, the training of cognitive skills: An interview with Alfred Binet. In S. Chipman, J. Segal, & R. Glaser (Eds.), *Thinking and learning skills. Vol. 2: Research and open questions* (pp. 319–337). Hillsdale, NJ: Lawrence Erlbaum Associates.

Bruner, J. (1973). *Beyond the information given: Studies in the psychology of knowing*. New York: W. W. Norton.

Cleary, P., & McNeil, B. (1988). Patient satisfaction as an indicator of quality care. *Inquiry, 25*(1), 25–36.

Covey, S. (1998). *The 7 habits of highly effective people*. New York: Free Press.

Daggett, W. (2009). Rigor and relevance: Preparing students for a 21st century world. *Seen*. Southeast Education Network. Available: http://seenmagazine.us/Articles/Article-Detail/articleid/207/rigor-and-relevance

Darling-Hammond, L., & Adamson, F. (2013). The next generation of assessments can—and must—be better. *ASCD Express: Ideas from the Field, 8*(18), 1.

Dusek, J. B., & Joseph, G. (1983). The bases of teacher expectancies: A meta-analysis. *Journal of Educational Psychology, 75*(3), 327–346.

Dweck, C. S. (2007). *Mindset: The new psychology of success*. New York: Ballantine Books.

Edmonds, R. (1979, October). Effective schools for the urban poor. *Educational Leadership.*

Finkelstein, N., Hanson, T., Huang, C.-W., Hirschman, B., & Huang, M. (2010). *Experimental study of BIE project-based economics units*. NCEE 2010–4022 rev U.S. Department of Education. Retrieved from https://ies.ed.gov/ncee/edlabs/regions/west/pdf/REL_20104022.pdf

Fisher, D., & Frey, N. (2016). *Gradual release of responsibility in the classroom.* (Quick Reference Guide). Alexandria, VA: ASCD.

Good, T. L. (1987). Two decades of research on teacher expectations: Findings and future. *Journal of Teacher Education, 38*(4), 32–47.

Goodrich, H. (1996, December/1997, January). Understanding rubrics. *Educational Leadership, 54*(4), 14–17.

Hattie, J. (2008). *Visible learning: A synthesis of over 800 meta-analyses relating to achievement.* New York: Routledge.

Hattie, J. (2013). *Visible learning for teachers: Maximizing impact on learning.* Thousand Oaks, CA: Corwin Press.

Haystead, M., & Marzano, R. (2009). *Meta-analytic synthesis of studies conducted at Marzano Research Laboratory on instructional strategies*. Englewood, CO: Marzano Research Laboratory.

Hiebert, N. M., Vo, A., Hampshire, A., Owen, A. M., Seergobin, K. N., & MacDonald, P. A. (2014). Striatum in stimulus response learning via feedback and in decision making. *Neuroimage, 101*, 448–457.

Karakowsky, L., & Mann, S. L. (2008). Setting goals and taking ownership: Understanding the implications of participatively set goals from a causal attribution perspective. *Journal of Leadership & Organizational Studies, 14*(3), 260–270.

Kuo, M., Paulus, W., & Nitsche, M. (2008). Boosting focally-induced brain plasticity by dopamine. *Cerebral Cortex, 18*(3), 648–651.

Lezotte, L. (2001). *Revolutionary and evolutionary: The effective schools movement.* Okemos, MI: Effective Schools Products.

Light, R. (2001). *Making the most out of college: Students speak their minds.* How should curriculum be reformatted? Cambridge, MA: Harvard University Press.

Luiten, J., Ames, W., & Ackerson, G. (1980). A meta-analysis of the effects of advance organizers on learning and retention. *American Educational Research Journal, 17*(2), 211–218.

Marshall, P., & Bredy, T. (2016). Cognitive neuroepigenetics: The next evolution in our understanding of the molecular mechanisms underlying learning and memory? *NPJ Science of Learning 1*, 16014.

Marzano, R. (1998). A theory-based meta-analysis of research on instruction. Denver: Mid-continent Regional Educational Laboratory.

Marzano, R., Pickering, D., & Pollock, J. (2001). *Classroom instruction that works: Research-based strategies for increasing student achievement.* Alexandria, VA: ASCD.

McTighe, J. (2013). *Core learning: Assessing what matters most.* Salt Lake City: School Improvement Network.

McTighe, J. (2016). Beware of the test prep trap. *Newsela Blog*. Retrieved from: https://blog.newsela.com/blog/2017/7/25/u2tlzoasa0gur7ua7uij7ihtop6dkp

McTighe, J., & O'Connor, K. (2005, November). Seven practices for effective learning. *Educational Leadership, 63*(3), 14.

McTighe, J., & Wiggins, G. (2013). *Essential questions: Opening doors to student understanding.* Alexandria, VA: ASCD.

Morisano, D., Hirsh, J., Peterson, J., Pihl, R., & Shore, B. (2010). Setting, elaborating, and reflecting on personal goals improves academic performance. *Journal of Applied Psychology, 95*(2), 255–264.

National Association of Colleges and Employers (NACE). (2016). Job Outlook 2016: The attributes employers want to see on new college graduates' resumes. Available: www.naceweb.org/s11182015/employers-look-for-in-new-hires.aspx

National Research Council. (2012). *Education for life and work: Developing transferable knowledge and skills in the 21st century.* Washington, DC: National Academies Press.

Peters, S., Braams, B., Raijmakers, M., Cedric, P., Koolschijn, M., & Crone, E. (2014). The neural coding of feedback learning across child and adolescent development. *Journal of Cognitive Neuroscience 26*(8), 1705–1720.

Piaget, J. (1957). *Construction of reality in the child.* London: Routledge & Kegan Paul.

Prabhakar, J., Coughlin, C., & Ghetti, S. (2016). The neurocognitive development of episodic prospection and its implications for academic achievement. *Mind, Brain, and Education: Memory Research Issue*, 196–206.

Richard, J. M., Castro, D. C., DiFeliceantonio, A. G., Robinson, M. J., & Berridge, K. C. (2013). Mapping brain circuits of reward and motivation: In the footsteps of Ann Kelley. *Neuroscience & Biobehavioral Reviews, 37*(9), 1919–1931.

Ross, M. (2016, March 7). School-based peer mentoring builds relationships, creates caring communities [blog post]. Retrieved from http://info.character.org/blog/school-based-peer-mentoring-builds-relationships

Silver, H., Strong, R., & Perini, M. (2007). *The strategic teacher: Selecting the right research-based strategy for every lesson.* Alexandria, VA: ASCD.

Spady, W. G. (1994). *Outcome-based education: Critical issues and answers.* Alexandria, VA: American Association of School Administrators.

Srinivasan, M. (2014). *Teach, breathe, learn.* Berkeley, CA: Parallax Press.

Stiggins, R. (1996). *Student-centered classroom assessment* (2nd ed.). New York: Prentice Hall.

Stiggins, R. (2004). *Student-involved assessment for learning.* Boston: Pearson.

Strauss, V. (2014a, June 9). How much Bill Gates's disappointing small-schools effort really cost. *Washington Post.* Retrieved from: www.washingtonpost.com/news/answer-sheet/wp/2014/10/24/teacher-spends-two-days-as-a-student-and-is-shocked-at-what-she-learned/?noredirect=on&utm_term=.65cca973c319

Strauss, V. (2014b, October 24). Teacher spends two days as a student and is shocked at what she learns. *Washington Post.* Retrieved from: www.washingtonpost.com/news/answer-sheet/wp/2014/10/24/teacher-spends-two-days-as-a-student-and-is-shocked-at-what-she-learned/?utm_term=.dd98662f0151

Tomlinson, C. A., & McTighe, J. (2006) *Differentiated instruction and Understanding by Design: Connecting content and kids.* Alexandria, VA: ASCD.

Tyler, R. (1948). *Basic principles of curriculum and instruction.* Chicago: University of Chicago Press.

United States Soccer Federation. (n.d.). *Best practices for coaching soccer in the United States.* Chicago: Author. Retrieved from www.ussoccer.com/~/media/migrated/documents/coaching/2009-to-2010/090903-best-practices-v2.pdf?la=en

van den Heuvel, M., Stam, C., Kahn, R., Hulshoff Pol, H. E. (2009). Efficiency of functional brain networks and intellectual performance. *Journal of Neuroscience, 29*(23), 7619–7624.

Varlas, L. (2018, June). Emotions are the rudder that steers thinking. *Education Update, 60*(6), 4. Available: www.ascd.org/publications/newsletters/education-update/jun18/vol60/num06/Emotions-Are-the-Rudder-That-Steers-Thinking.aspx

Vygotsky, L. S. (1978). Interaction between learning and development (M. Lopez-Morillas, Trans.). In M. Cole, V. John-Steiner, S. Scribner, & E. Souberman (Eds.), *Mind in society: The development of higher psychological processes* (pp. 79–91). Cambridge, MA: Harvard University Press.

Wiggins, G. (2006, April 3). Healthier testing made easy: The idea of authentic assessment. *Edutopia*. Retrieved from www.edutopia.org/authentic-assessment-grant-wiggins

Wiggins, G. (2012, September). Seven keys to effective feedback. *Educational Leadership, 70*(1), 10–16.

Wiggins, G., & McTighe, J. (2004). *The Understanding by Design professional development workbook*. Alexandria, VA: ASCD.

Wiggins, G., & McTighe, J. (2011). *The Understanding by Design guide to creating high-quality units.* Alexandria, VA: ASCD.

Wiggins, G., & McTighe, J. (2012). *The Understanding by Design guide to advanced concepts in creating and reviewing units.* Alexandria, VA: ASCD.

Willis, J. (2006). *Research-based strategies to ignite student learning: Insights from a neurologist /classroom teacher*. Alexandria, VA: ASCD.

Willis, J. (2009a, April 22). Your brain owner's manual: A guide to getting the most out of your brain [blog post]. Retrieved from www.psychologytoday.com/us/blog/radical-teaching/200904/your-brain-owners-manual

Willis, J. (2009b, December/2010, January). How to teach students about the brain. *Educational Leadership, 67*(4). Retrieved from www.ascd.org/publications/educational-leadership/dec09/vol67/num04/How-to-Teach-Students-About-the-Brain.aspx

Willis, J. (2009c). What you should know about your brain. *Educational Leadership*. Retrieved from www.ascd.org/ASCD/pdf/journals/ed_lead/el200912_willis.pdf

Wong, H., Wong, R., Rogers, K., & Brooks, A. (2012). Managing your classroom for success. *Science and Children, 49*(9), 60.

Index

Note: The letter *d* following a page locator denotes a definition, the letter *f* denotes a figure.

About the Authors

Jay McTighe brings a wealth of experience from a rich and varied career in education. He served as director of the Maryland Assessment Consortium, a collaboration of school districts working together to develop and share formative performance assessments. Previously he was involved with school improvement projects at the Maryland State Department of Education, where he helped lead standards-based reforms, including development of performance-based statewide assessments. He directed development of the Instructional Framework, a multimedia database on teaching. Well known for his work with thinking skills, Jay coordinated statewide efforts to develop instructional strategies, curriculum models, and assessment procedures for improving the quality of student thinking. In addition to his work at the state level, Jay has experience at the district level in Prince George's County, Maryland, as a classroom teacher, resource specialist, and program coordinator. He also directed a state residential enrichment program for gifted and talented students.

Jay is an accomplished author, having coauthored 16 books, including the award-winning and best-selling *Understanding by Design* series with Grant Wiggins. His books have been translated into six languages. Jay has also written more than 35 articles and book chapters, and has been published in leading journals, including *Educational Leadership* and *Education Week*.

With an extensive background in professional development, Jay is a regular speaker at national, state, and district conferences and workshops. He has made presentations in 47 states within the United States, in 7 Canadian provinces, and internationally to educators in 37 countries on six continents.

Jay received his undergraduate degree from the College of William and Mary, earned his master's degree from the University of Maryland, and completed postgraduate studies at the Johns Hopkins University. He was selected to participate in the Educational Policy Fellowship Program through the Institute for Educational Leadership in Washington, D.C., and served as a member of the National Assessment Forum, a coalition of education and civil rights organizations advocating reforms in national, state, and local assessment policies and practices. Jay may be reached via e-mail at jay@mctighe-associates.com and on Twitter @jaymctighe. His website is www.jaymactighe.com.

After graduating Phi Beta Kappa as the first woman graduate from Williams College, Judy Willis attended the UCLA School of Medicine, where she was awarded her medical degree. She remained at UCLA and completed a medical residency and neurology residency, including chief residency. She practiced neurology for 15 years before returning to university to obtain her teaching credential and master's of education from the University of California, Santa Barbara. She has taught in elementary and middle school for the past 10 years.

An authority on brain research regarding learning and the brain, Judy writes extensively for professional educational journals and has written a number of books about applying brain and education research to classroom teaching. In 2007 the Association of Educational Publishers honored her as a finalist for the Distinguished Achievement Award for her educational writing.

Judy is a presenter at educational conferences and conducts professional development workshops nationally and internationally about classroom strategies correlated with neuroscience research, and she has been a Distinguished and Featured Presenter at ASCD national conferences. Her books include *Research-Based Strategies to Ignite Student Learning, Brain-Friendly Strategies for the Inclusion Classroom, Teaching the*

Brain to Read, Inspiring Middle School Minds, How Your Child Learns Best, Learning to Love Math, Unlock Your Teen's Brainpower, and *The Neuroscience of Learning: Principles and Applications for Educators.* Contact Judy through her website at www.RADTeach.com and follow her on Twitter @judywillis.

Related ASCD Resources: Brain and Learning

At the time of publication, the following resources were available (ASCD stock numbers in parentheses). For up-to-date information about ASCD resources, go to www.ascd.org. You can search the complete archives of *Educational Leadership* at www.ascd.org/el.

Print Products

Attack of the Teenage Brain! Understanding and Supporting the Weird and Wonderful Adolescent Learner, by John Medina (#118024)

Engage the Brain: How to Design for Learning That Taps into the Power of Emotion, by Allison Posey (#119015)

Essential Questions: Opening Doors to Student Understanding, by Jay McTighe and Grant Wiggins (#109004)

How to Teach So Students Remember, 2nd ed., by Marilee Sprenger (#118016)

Making the Most of Understanding by Design, by John L. Brown (#103110)

The Power of the Adolescent Brain: Strategies for Teaching Middle and High School Students, by Thomas Armstrong (#116017)

Research-Based Strategies to Ignite Student Learning: Insights from a Neurologist and Classroom Teacher, by Judy Willis (#107006)

Teaching Students to Drive Their Brains: Metacognitive Strategies, Activities, and Lesson Ideas, by Donna Wilson and Marcus Conyers (#117002)

The Understanding by Design Guide to Advanced Concepts in Creating and Reviewing Units by Grant Wiggins and Jay McTighe (#112026)

The Understanding by Design Guide to Creating High-Quality Units, by Grant Wiggins and Jay McTighe (#109107)

ASCD myTeachSource®

Download resources from a professional learning platform with hundreds of research-based best practices and tools for your classroom at http://myteachsource.ascd.org/.

For more information, send an e-mail to member@ascd.org; call 1-800-933-2723 or 703-578-9600; send a fax to 703-575-5400; or write to Information Services, ASCD, 1703 N. Beauregard St., Alexandria, VA 22311-1714 USA.